W9-DIL-003

Katherine J. Creagh
August 13, 2008

Archbishop Fulton Sheen's
St. Thérèse

A TREASURED LOVE STORY

Fulton J. Sheen

2007

Copyright © 2007 Basilica Press
All rights reserved

Published by Basilica Press
111 Fergus Court, Ste. 102
Irving, TX 75062

The editors have endeavoured to preserve to the greatest extent possible Archbishop Sheen's words as he spoke them. However, there were places where the editors made slight, non-substantive adjustments for the sake of clarity and greater readability.

Except for brief excerpts in articles or critical reviews, no part of this book may be reproduced, transmitted, or stored in any form by any means, electronic, mechanical, recorded, photocopy, or otherwise, without prior permission in writing from the copyright owner.

The Scripture verses herein are taken from several translations as Archbishop Sheen quoted from a number of different versions.

Photos of St. Thérèse © Office Central de Lisieux
Photos of Archbishop Fulton Sheen © Diocese of Rochester, NY

Editors: Fr. Andrew Apostoli, CFR, Carolyn Klika, and
                    Brian O'Neel

Interior Design: Giuliana Gerber, ACI Prensa

Cover design: Ted Schluenderfritz, Five Sparrows Media
                   (www.5sparrows.com)

Printed in the United States of America
ISBN 978-1-930314-09-2

Basilica Press is part of the Joseph and Marie Daou Foundation

Table of Contents

Introduction

This book is meant to celebrate something very special in the Church.

On December 14, 1927, Pope Pius XI proclaimed St. Thérèse of the Child Jesus principal patroness of all missions and all missionaries, the equal to St. Francis Xavier.[A]

In 2007, the entire Catholic world will celebrate the eightieth anniversary of that happy event with great solemnity. The Shrine of St. Thérèse in Lisieux and the Lisieux Carmel have, in fact, already begun their commemorations.

I mention this fact for two reasons:

1. St. Thérèse, much as she would have loved to, never set foot on mission soil, and yet she most powerfully helped the missions by her

heroic prayer and sacrifices. The Pope wanted to highlight this fact and to remind us that we, too, could and should do likewise.

2. The Servant of God Archbishop Fulton Sheen, whose great love was the Catholic missions, was also very aware of the missionary power of Carmelite contemplatives such as St. Thérèse. In fact, his life-long correspondence with the Carmelite Sisters in New Albany, Indiana, is fully reserved in his Rochester archives. Very revealingly, he wrote to the Carmelite prioress, *"Your prayers and sufferings do more good than all our preaching and our hectic actions. We make the noise; we get the credit; we enjoy the consolation of a victory seen and tasted. You are responsible for it and yet you cannot see the fruits— but you will, on that day when the Cross appears in the heavens and every man is rewarded according to his works."* He also wrote, *"I want to cling on to Carmel for I love its love of Jesus. I refuse to give it up, and like the blind man of Jericho, I shall go on shouting out to you continually to cure my blindness and my ills."*

In 1973, the centenary of St. Thérèse's birth, I was anxious that we would celebrate this "greatest saint of modern times" in the best possible way. Given his great love of the missions (he was director of the Society of the

Propagation of the Faith[1] for 16 years) and the fact that he was a professed member of the Carmelite Third Order and easily the most renowned preacher in the world of his time, I felt Archbishop Sheen was the one to invite to preach, if he had the availability. He had already preached on two special occasions in our Carmelite Church at Whitefriar Street, Dublin (1969 and 1971), and we were thrilled when he accepted our request to preach on St. Thérèse.

For me, the novena he preached was unforgettable. My only regret is that the 11 beautiful sermons he gave were never put into book form until now. For their publication I owe a deep debt of gratitude to Fr. Andrew Apostoli, CFR, vice-postulator of Archbishop Sheen's cause for canonization. It was totally his idea that these splendid talks be published, and he has done all the work to bring this brilliant jewel to light.

These beautiful talks are vintage Sheen. His approach to St. Thérèse is absolutely unique. It is abundantly clear that he is a master of her spirituality, and that his own spiritual life drew much inspiration from her. Principally using her autobiography *Story of a Soul* (written under the patronage of Our Blessed Lady, for whom both St. Thérèse and the archbishop had a most tender love), he takes us through her beautiful life and that spiritual classic in a masterful way.

---

1 According to the online *Catholic Encyclopedia*, "This society is an international association for the assistance by prayers and alms of Catholic missionary priests, brothers, and nuns engaged in preaching the Gospel in ... non-Catholic countries." Sheen was director of its American branch. Between 1950 and 1966, he raised $200 million for foreign missions. In today's dollars, that would roughly equate to $1.172 billion.

He gives us precious insights into her virtues, her faith, hope, charity, fortitude, and humility, her heroic perseverance in prayer, her science of divine love, her heroic resistance to the temptations to suicide, not to mention her total grasp of God's teaching and its application to our everyday lives. He was fascinated by her love for and knowledge of sacred Scripture (attributes that could similarly be ascribed to him).

He even gives us a count of St. Thérèse's quotations (107 from the Old Testament and 250 from the New Testament). Archbishop Sheen adds, "Think of that! One hundred and seven from the Old. And she did not study Scripture as the scholar does. For example, she picked up the Prophet Isaiah and she read, she said, about 50 chapters before there came to her an inspiration that she applied to her own life."

I find in taking up this book that it makes for compelling reading—a reluctance to put it down. Not only does it reveal the essential Thérèse, it also reveals the essential Fulton Sheen. This is a book that will be a rich resource for anyone's spiritual reading or meditation and, extraordinarily, it is as relevant to today's spiritual life as it was when first delivered 33 years ago. It is no wonder St. Thérèse is called "one of the ageless saints of God." Needless to add, it is written with all the famous Sheen wit and charm.

St. Thérèse has been greatly misunderstood by many who have attempted to interpret her. One of the greatest communicators of the twentieth century, the Servant of

God Archbishop Sheen has not made that mistake but has left us a wonderfully readable book that directs and authentically leads us in the footsteps of St. Thérèse. He has dealt very lucidly with her great power of intercession.

May the Little Flower take special care of Fulton Sheen's cause for canonization.

To Fr. Andrew Apostoli, his staff, and to all who read these majestic sermons, may St. Thérèse send her choicest roses.

Fr. J. Linus Ryan, O. Carm.
St. Thérèse National Office,
Carmelite Community,
Terenure College,
Dublin 6W, Ireland
October 1, 2006,
Feast of St. Thérèse of the Child Jesus
of the Holy Face

∽❦∾

Notes

A. *Quam laeto animi,* declaration, Sacred Congregation of Rites, December 14, 1927, *Acta Apostolicae Sedis,* 20, pgs. 147-8.

Foreward

When the possibility arose of transcribing the novena talks that Archbishop Fulton J. Sheen preached on the occasion of the one-hundredth anniversary of the birth of St. Thérèse of Lisieux, I thought about a story involving two saints.

The two saints were the Dominican St. Thomas Aquinas and the Franciscan St. Bonaventure of Bagnaregio. They were contemporaries, good friends, and both became Doctors of the Church.

Now the story tells us how St. Bonaventure went to the famous hermitage called Mount Alvernia in central Italy, the same mountain where St. Francis of Assisi received the *stigmata* (i.e., the five wounds of Christ crucified) in his hands, feet, and side. It was a very holy place of prayer. St. Bonaventure had gone there to write a biography of St. Francis, the founder of his Order.

The story goes on to tell us that St. Thomas Aquinas came by Mount Alvernia one day with some of his Dominican companions, and he wanted to visit with St. Bonaventure. When a Franciscan friar went to notify St. Bonaventure about his visitors, the friar found the saint in a prayerful state of ecstasy. When told of this, St. Thomas is said to have remarked to his companions, "Let us leave one saint to write about another!"

In our present case, we have one canonized person (St. Thérèse of Lisieux) and another, God willing, on the road to canonization (the Servant of God Archbishop Fulton J. Sheen). If, as an old expression puts it, "It takes one to know one," then this treatment of the life of St. Thérèse will be exceptionally blessed.

Archbishop Sheen, with his own profound wisdom, insight, and personal holiness, uniquely explores the depths of holiness of this "saint of the Little Way." He reveals the secrets of this "greatest saint of modern times," as Pope St. Pius X called her. These secrets of holiness were so hidden that, as her death approached (and knowing they would have to notify the neighboring Carmelite monasteries of her death while sharing a brief summary of her life), two of her fellow nuns remarked, "What are we going to write about Thérèse? She never did *anything*!!"

Well, for a nun who never did "anything," it was said that in the first 100 years after her death, 900 books were written about the saint from Lisieux. Because of this, some people may ask, "Is there a need for *another* work on St. Thérèse?"

We can only reply, "Read the book!" You will be moved and inspired by what such a great evangelist as Archbishop Fulton J. Sheen has to tell us about this extremely popular saint! After all, it is a book written about a saint by a potential saint. No one can better explain what is happening than someone who has been there! The names, dates, places, and situations in the lives of saintly people may change, but the daily dying with Christ and the daily rising with Christ on the road to sanctity are basically the same!

Thus, The Archbishop Fulton J. Sheen Foundation is honored and delighted to make this present work available to the Church, especially to the many devoted followers of both the "Little Flower" and Archbishop Fulton J. Sheen.

The Foundation is extremely grateful to Fr. J. Linus Ryan, O. Carm. (the Carmelite priest from Dublin who invited the archbishop to preach the novena) for his permission to transcribe the beautifully preached novena into a book. This will allow the message about St. Thérèse to reach an even greater number of people in written format.

Finally, the Foundation thanks Basilica Press for printing this volume, which will serve as a spiritual guide for many. In particular, the Foundation wishes to acknowledge the work of final editing done by Carolyn Klika and Brian O'Neel, Kathleen Wilson for her research help, Ted Schleunderfritz for his cover design, and Giuliana Gerber for her interior design work. We also thank the Carmelite Convent of Lisieux and Sr. Cindy with the

Archives of the Diocese of Rochester for helping us procuring the photos herein. Furthermore, the Foundation wishes to acknowledge the work of Elaine Curzio, ocds, who transcribed the text, and Catherine Dillon, who did the initial editing. Finally, the Foundation acknowledges the dedicated work of Alan Napleton of the Catholic Marketing Network (CMN), who initiated the process of publishing along with help from others at CMN, especially Pamela Presbitero and Kate Jasmin.

Father Andrew Apostoli, CFR
Vice Postulator of Archbishop Sheen's Cause

The Life of St. Thérèse of Lisieux

by Fr. J. Linus Ryan, O. Carm.

St. Thérèse of Lisieux, known to millions as "the Little Flower," is one of the greatest spiritual teachers in the history of the Catholic Church. That is why so many popes have held her up as a model and, indeed, why the Servant of God Archbishop Fulton Sheen—the supreme communicator of the twentieth century—had a similar interest in her.

Pope Pius XI, who considered Thérèse of Lisieux the "star of my pontificate," did not hesitate to assert in his homily on May 17, 1925, the day of her canonization, that, "The Spirit of truth opened and made known to her what He usually hides from the wise and prudent and reveals to little ones; thus she enjoyed such knowledge of the things above—as Our immediate Predecessor Benedict XV attests—that she shows everyone else the sure way of salvation."[1]

The Servant of God Pope John Paul II said we can apply to Thérèse of Lisieux what his predecessor the Servant of God Pope Paul VI said of another young saint and Doctor of the Church, Catherine of Siena:

> "'What strikes us most about the saint is her infused wisdom, that is to say, her lucid, profound, and inebriating absorption of the divine truths and mysteries of faith... That assimilation was certainly favored by the most singular natural gifts, but it was also evidently something prodigious, due to a charism of wisdom from the Holy Spirit.'"[2]

Earlier in this same talk John Paul II had said:

> "In a time like ours, so frequently marked by an ephemeral and hedonistic culture, [St. Thérèse] proves to be remarkably effective in enlightening the mind and heart of those who hunger and thirst for truth and love."[3]

Her Life

St. Thérèse of the Child Jesus was born Thérèse

---

1 *Vehementer exultamus hodie*, Pius XI, "Bull of Canonization of St. Thérèse of the Child Jesus and the Holy Face."
2 Homily of John Paul II at the proclamation of St. Thérèse of the Child Jesus and the Holy Face as a Doctor of the Church, Sunday, October 19, 1997, http://www.vatican.va/holy_father/john_paul_ii/homilies/1997/documents/hf_jp-ii_hom_19101997_en.html
3 ibid.

Martin in Alençon, Normandy, France, on January 2, 1873, and was baptized two days later in the Church of Notre Dame, receiving the name Marie-Françoise-Thérèse. Her parents were the Venerable Zélie (née Guérin) and the Venerable Louis Martin (both of whom, hopefully, will soon be beatified as model parents). After her mother's death on August 28, 1877, the Martin family moved to the town of Lisieux where, surrounded by the affection of her father and sisters, Thérèse received a formation both demanding and full of tenderness.

Towards the end of 1879, she received the Sacrament of Penance for the first time. On Pentecost 1883, she had the extraordinary grace of being healed from a serious illness through the intercession of Our Lady of Victory. Educated by the Benedictines of Lisieux, she received First Communion on May 8, 1884. This followed an intense period of preparation and was crowned by an exceptional experience of the grace of intimate union with Jesus.

A few weeks later on June 14, she received the Sacrament of Confirmation. She did so with a vivid awareness of what the coming of the Holy Spirit meant to her personally: "Particularly on that day I received the strength to suffer, for soon afterwards the martyrdom of my soul was about to commence."[4]

On Christmas 1886, she had a profound spiritual experience that she subsequently described as a "complete conversion." As a result, she overcame the emotional

---

4 Manuscript A, Chapter IV, p. 80

weakness caused by the loss of her mother and on Christmas 1886, she had a profound spiritual experience that she subsequently described as a "complete conversion." As a result, she overcame the emotional weakness caused by the loss of her mother and began "to run as a giant" on the way of perfection.

Thérèse wished to embrace the contemplative life in the Carmel of Lisieux, like her sisters Pauline and Marie. She was prevented from doing so, however, on account of her young age. On November 20, 1887, during a pilgrimage to Italy, she and her fellow pilgrims were given an audience with Pope Leo XIII (1878-1903). With filial boldness, she took the opportunity to ask His Holiness to enter Carmel at age 15. (Archbishop Sheen reveals the answer Leo gave later in this book.)

On April 9, 1888, she entered the Lisieux Carmel, where she received the habit of the Blessed Virgin's order[5] on January 10 of the following year, and made her religious profession on September 8, 1890, the feast of the Birth of the Virgin Mary. At Carmel, she undertook the way of perfection marked out by the Mother Foundress St. Teresa of Jesus[6] with genuine fervor and fidelity in fulfilling the various community tasks entrusted to her.

Enlightened by the word of God, and tried in

---

5 Editor's note: From its earliest days, the Carmelite Order has been known as the Sacred Order of the Blessed Virgin Mary of Mount Carmel, for the Carmelites not only credited Our Lady with founding the Order but with its continual preservation. Hence, "the Blessed Virgin's order."
6 Aka, St. Teresa of Avila.

particular by the illness of her beloved father Ven. Louis
Martin (who died on July 29, 1894), Thérèse embarked
on the way of holiness, insisting on the *centrality of love*.
She discovered and imparted to the novices entrusted
to her care "the Little Way of Spiritual Childhood." The
Little Way was the means she used to enter more and more
deeply into the mystery of the Church. As a result of this,
and drawn by the love of Christ, she felt growing within
her the apostolic and missionary vocation that spurred her
to bring everyone with her to meet the Divine Spouse.

On June 9, 1895, the Feast of the Most Holy Trinity,
she offered herself as a sacrificial victim to the Merciful
Love of God. On April 3 of the following year, on the
night between Holy Thursday and Good Friday, she
noticed the first symptoms of the illness which led to her
death. Thérèse welcomed this as a mysterious visitation of
the Divine Spouse. At the same time, she underwent a trial
of faith that lasted until her death.

As her health deteriorated, she was moved to the
infirmary. Her sisters and other religious collected her
sayings, while her sufferings and trials, borne with patience,
intensified until the moment of her death on the afternoon
of September 30, 1897. Her last words, "My God, I love
You," are the seal of her life.

"I am not dying; I am entering life," she had written
Fr. Bellière, one of her spiritual brothers (Lettres 244). And
so she did.

Her Writings

Thérèse of the Child of Jesus left us writings that deservedly qualified her as a teacher of the spiritual life. Her principal work remained the account of her life in three autobiographical manuscripts (*Manuscritis autobiographiques A, B, C*) published under the title of *Histoire d'une Âme* (Story of a Soul).

Written at the request of her sister Mother Agnes of Jesus, prioress of the monastery, and given to Mother on January 21, 1896, Manuscript A described the stages of her religious experience: the early years of childhood (especially the time of her First Communion and Confirmation); adolescence; her entrance into Carmel; and her first profession.

Considered by many as the jewel of her writings, Manuscript B was written during her retreat that same year at the request of her sister Marie of the Sacred Heart. It contained some of the most beautiful, best known, and oft-quoted passages from the saint of Lisieux. They revealed the Little Flower's full maturity as she spoke of her vocation in the Church, the Bride of Christ and Mother of souls.

Manuscript C was composed in June and the first days of July 1897, a few months before her death, and was dedicated to Prioress Marie de Gonzague, who had requested it.[7] It completed the recollections in Manuscript A regarding life in Carmel.

---

7 Mother Marie succeeded Mother Agnes as prioress.

These pages revealed the author's supernatural wisdom. Thérèse recounted some sublime experiences during this final period of her life. She devoted moving pages to her trial of faith. This trial brought with it a grace of purification that immersed her in a long and painful dark night, one that was only illuminated by her trust in God's merciful, fatherly love.[8]

Thus in this third set of reflections, without repeating herself, Thérèse again made the Gospel's light shine brightly. Here we find the most beautiful pages she devoted to trusting abandonment into God's hands, to the unity that exists between love of God and love of neighbor, and to her missionary vocation in the Church.

While different from one another, this trinity of manuscripts converge in a thematic unity and provide a progressive description of her life and spiritual way. As such, Thérèse has left us an original autobiography that is indeed the story of her soul. It shows how God has offered the world a precise message: Through her, He shows us an evangelical way, the "Little Way," which everyone can take because everyone is called to holiness.

---

8 *Grace of purification* is a common term used by all the mystics to describe part of the process that leads them to holiness. A number of the saints comment on how trials, disappointments, crosses of various kinds, and aridity in prayer, all accepted in the right spirit, help to *purify the soul* of sins and imperfections. St. Thérèse is no exception. She regards her *great trial of faith*, to which she devotes 25 of the 52 pages of Manuscript C, as "*a grace of purification*." "The long and painful dark night" is a direct referral to her *trial of faith*. Incidentally, I might add that these 25 pages are some of the most moving Thérèse wrote. What many people don't realise is that she even experienced strong temptations to commit suicide during this period.

She also wrote at least 266 *lettres* to family members, women religious, and missionary "brothers." In these, Thérèse shares her wisdom, developing a teaching that is actually a profound exercise in the spiritual direction of souls.

Additionally, her writings also include 54 *poésies*,[9] some of which have great theological and spiritual depth inspired by Sacred Scripture. Worthy of special mention are *Vivre d'Amour!*[10] and *Pour-quoi je t'aime, ò Marie!*[11] an original synthesis of the Virgin Mary's journey according to the Gospel. To this literary production should be added eight *récréations pieuses*,[12] poetic and theatrical compositions the saint conceived and performed for her community on certain feast days in accordance with the tradition of Carmel. Among those writings should be mentioned a series of 21 *prières*.[13] Nor can we forget the collection of all she said during the last months of her life. These sayings, known as the *Novissima verba* and of which there are several editions, have also been given the title *Derniers Entretiens*.[14]

Her Legacy

The reception given to the example of her life and Gospel teaching in our century was quick, universal, and

---

9 French for "poems."
10 *Living on Love! Poésies* 17
11 *Why I love you, O Mary! Poésies* 54
12 *Pious Recreations*
13 *Prayers*
14 *Last Conversations*

constant. As if in imitation of her precocious spiritual maturity, her holiness was recognized by the Church in the space of a few years. In fact, on June 10, 1914, St. Pius X signed the decree introducing her Cause of Beatification. On August 14, 1921, Benedict XV declared the heroic virtues of the Servant of God, giving an address for the occasion on *The Way of Spiritual Childhood*; Pius XI beatified her on April 19, 1923.

Just two years later, afterwards, on May 17, 1925, the same Pope canonized her before an immense crowd in the Basilica of St. Peter, highlighting the splendor of her virtues and the originality of her doctrine. A short time later, on December 14, 1927, in response to the petition of many missionary bishops, he proclaimed her patron of the missions along with St. Francis Xavier.[15]

Beginning with these acts of recognition, the spiritual radiance of Thérèse of the Child Jesus increased in the Church and spread throughout the world.

- Many institutes of consecrated life and ecclesial movements, especially in the young Churches, chose her as their patron and teacher, taking their inspiration from her spiritual doctrine.

- Her message, often summarized in the so-called "Little Way," which is nothing other than the Gospel way of holiness for all, was studied by theologians and experts in spirituality.

---

15 He also made her patroness of the Society of St. Peter the Apostle and of Mexico.

25

- Cathedrals, basilicas, shrines, and churches throughout the world were built and dedicated to the Lord under the patronage of the saint of Lisieux.

- The Catholic Church venerated her in the various Eastern and Western rites.

- Uncountable numbers of the faithful were able to experience the power of her intercession.

- Many of those called to the priestly ministry or the consecrated life, especially in the missions and the cloister, attributed the divine grace of their vocation to her intercession and example.

The Supreme Pontiffs of the twentieth century, all of whom held up her holiness as a universal example, each stressed that Thérèse was a teacher of the spiritual life with a doctrine both spiritual and profound. This she drew from the Gospel sources under the guidance of the Divine Teacher and then imparted what she had learned to her brothers and sisters in the Church with the greatest effectiveness.[16]

This spiritual doctrine was passed on to us primarily via her autobiography *Story of a Soul*, and it has aroused an extraordinary interest down to our day. This book, translated along with her other writings into about 70 languages, has made Thérèse known in every part of the world, even outside the Catholic Church.

---

16 Cf. Manuscript B, 2v°-3v°

Thus, more than a century after her death, Thérèse of the Child Jesus and the Holy Face continues to be recognized as one of the great masters of the spiritual life in our time.

The Life of Archbishop Fulton J. Sheen

by Fr. Andrew Apostoli, CFR

His Early Years

Archbishop Fulton J. Sheen was born to Newton and Delia (née Fulton) Sheen, on May 8, 1895, in El Paso, Illinois. This oldest of four sons was baptized Peter John, but growing up became known by his mother's maiden name, Fulton, a name he favored. At his baptism, his mother dedicated him to the Blessed Virgin Mary, and he renewed this dedication at his First Holy Communion. Attending Catholic grammar and high schools in Peoria, Illinois, he always showed keen interest in reading rather than doing manual work on his father's farm. He later attended St. Viator College in Bourbonnais, Illinois, where he laid the groundwork for his future preaching and writing by joining the school's debate team and newspaper staff.

Not surprisingly, Sheen was an excellent student,

and he earned a significant scholarship for advanced studies after graduation. He turned this down, however, to follow his desire to become a priest. He was ordained to the priesthood on September 20, 1919.

It was during his years of study at St. Paul Seminary in St. Paul, MN, that Sheen learned the story that was to effect his priesthood forever. It was that of a young Chinese girl's heroic love for Jesus in the Holy Eucharist. Because of her example, he made his famous promise to spend a "Holy Hour" each day before Jesus in the Blessed Sacrament, a promise he kept faithfully throughout his whole priestly life.[A]

After ordination, he first pursued post-graduate studies at Catholic University of America (CUA) in Washington, DC. From there he went on to the University of Louvain in Belgium, where he completed requirements for his doctorate in Philosophy. He was then invited to apply for the highly respected *agrégé* degree in Philosophy, which he received with outstanding distinction.[B] During this time, he also studied at the Sorbonne in Paris and the Angelicum in Rome. Subsequently, he taught Dogmatic Theology at St. Edmund's College near Ware, England (1925). He was to receive many honorary degrees and distinguished awards throughout his long and fruitful life.

When he returned to the United States, his bishop, Edward Michael Dunne (1909-29), feared the young priest's fame and success in Europe might have filled him with pride. So to test him, His Excellency sent Sheen to St. Patrick Church, a parish in inner-city Peoria. Within nine months, the young priest's pastoral dedication and dynamic sermons had turned St. Patrick's into a thriving parish. Bishop Dunne then assigned him to CUA's faculty, where he taught Theology, Philosophy, and Religion for 24 years (1926-1950).

His Years as a Media Pioneer

His fame and influence as a preacher, writer, and teacher of the Faith began to grow immensely. All forms of media were available to him. In 1926, he began his first radio programs from an always overcrowded Church of St. Paul in Manhattan. These talks were broadcast in the New York City area. Later, people nationwide heard him through his "Catholic Hour" broadcasts on NBC (1930-1952), which ultimately reached an estimated listening audience of four million every Sunday afternoon. These broadcasts had a solidly Catholic content.

His greatest success in media, however, came when he went on television with his series, "Life is Worth Living" (1952-1957), first broadcast on the DuMont Television Network and then ABC. Despite being opposite the very popular Milton Berle (aka, "Mr. Television"), the archbishop's weekly viewing audience grew to an estimated 30 million people and earned him an Emmy as Most Outstanding Television Personality in just his second year. These TV shows were more general in content than his radio programs, since many of his viewers were not Catholic. Many focused on the threat of communism, and during one, he is believed to have predicted the death of Soviet dictator Joseph Stalin.

Through this time, he was doing a great deal of writing, authoring 64 books and 65 pamphlets, as well as two weekly newspaper columns and a huge amount of personal correspondence. One result of all this "media evangelization" was that he attracted large numbers of converts to the Catholic Faith. They included the rich and famous, like Clare Booth Luce and Henry Ford II, as well as a great number of ordinary people.

In 1950, the archbishop's work began to take a new direction. He was appointed the national director of the Society for the Propagation of the Faith, a position he held until 1966. His popularity was a great asset, helping him to raise large amounts of money for the support of the Church's foreign missions (he even donated from his own TV salary and upwards of $10 million over the course of his public life, an amount that would equate to $62 million in today's dollars). As he would often say, "My greatest love has always been the Missions of the Church." With Bl. John XXIII, he co-consecrated several missionary bishops in 1960 and 1961. He was also to become the first Latin rite bishop ever to offer a solemn Byzantine rite Mass in English.

His Later Years

He participated in Vatican Council II (1962-1965) and was appointed to the Commission on the Missions by Pope Paul VI. His insights on the missions as well as on the importance of the role of women in the changing world were very farsighted. In 1966, Pope Paul VI appointed him bishop for the Diocese of Rochester, NY, a position he held for three years, when, at age 75, he submitted his resignation to Pope Paul VI. As he put it, "I am not retiring, only re-treading!" The Pope then named him archbishop of the titular See of Newport, Wales.[c] He spent his last years preaching and writing. Near the end of his life, he experienced tremendously painful suffering due to heart trouble. God took him to his eternal reward on December 9, 1979.

The impact of his life was summed up in the beautiful words with which Pope John Paul II greeted him in New York's St. Patrick Cathedral on October 2, 1979: "You have written and spoken well of the Lord Jesus! You have been a loyal son of the Church!"

✣

Notes

A. According to the Cardinal Kung Foundation, the story is this:

"There was a little Chinese girl of 11 years. When the Communists took over China, they imprisoned her parish pastor in his own rectory near the church.

"After they locked him up, the priest was horrified

to look out of his window and see the Communists proceed into the church. There they went into the sanctuary and broke into the tabernacle. In an act of hateful desecration, they took the ciborium and threw it on the floor, with all of the Sacred Hosts spilling out. The priest knew exactly how many Hosts were in the ciborium: 32.

"When the Communists left, they either did not notice, or didn't pay any attention to a small girl praying in the back of the church. She saw everything that had happened.

"Late that night, the little girl came back. Slipping past the guard at the priest's house, she went inside the Church. There she made a holy hour of prayer, an act of love to make up for the act of hatred.

After her holy hour she went into the sanctuary, knelt down, bent over, and, with her tongue, received Jesus in Holy Communion (since it was not permissible at that time for laypersons to touch the Sacred Host with their hands).

"The little girl continued to come back each night to make her holy hour and receive Jesus in Holy Communion on her tongue. On the thirty-second night, after she had consumed the last and thirty-second Host, she accidentally made a noise and woke the sleeping guard. He ran after her, caught her, and beat her to death with the butt of his rifle.

"This act of heroic martyrdom was witnessed by the grief-stricken priest as he watched from his bedroom window."

However, it may not have been the communists who perpetrated this terrible crime.

According to Fr. Andrew Apostoli, CFR, he spoke

with a bishop at an EWTN event. This bishop told him he had spoken with a seminary classmate of Sheen's at St. Paul Seminary, who said he, Sheen, and another classmate heard this story while they were students there.

Sheen entered St. Paul's in 1917 and received ordination in 1919. Chinese Communists were not a force at this time. Indeed, Mao Zedong, the man who led China into communism, was just then learning of communist principles. Zhou Enlai, arguably the second most important person in the history of Chinese communism, did not become a communist until after Sheen was already a priest. The first congress of Chinese communists did not take place until 1921. Communism as a movement during this period, therefore, if not in its infancy, was at least in its "toddlerhood." It certainly did not have the wherewithal to foment revolution or to even produce armed forces capable of doing something like what we read about above (Of course, it did things very much like this after the 1948 revolution, and Chinese communism made – and continues to make – many martyrs).

So if we are to take Sheen's classmate at his word (and there is no reason not to), this incident must have occurred during the 1911 Republican Revolution or, more likely, during the Boxer Rebellion (1899-1901), which was more focused on attacking anything smacking of foreign influence and was much more brutal.

In any event, the story so inspired Bishop Sheen, that he promised God to make a holy hour of prayer before Jesus in the Blessed Sacrament everyday for the rest of his life. After all, if this little Chinese girl could risk her life everyday to express her love for Jesus in the Blessed Sacrament with a holy hour and Holy Communion, then, at the very least, the bishop thought he should do the same.

His sole desire from then on was to bring the world to the Burning Heart of Jesus in the Blessed Sacrament.

The little girl showed the bishop what true courage and zeal really is, how faith could overcome all fear, and how true love for Jesus in the Eucharist must transcend life itself.

B.   There is nothing comparable to the *agrégé* degree in the United States. Some have described it as a sort of "super-doctorate." The word "agrégé" means incorporated, and by earning the degree, one becomes incorporated or "aggregated" to a European university faculty. Evidently, it is tradition to receive a dinner after sitting for one's agrégé. You could tell how successful a person was in passing the exam by the beverage they served at dinner. If you did satisfactorily, they served you water. If you passed with distinction, they served you beer. If you passed with great distinction, they gave you wine, and if you passed with the very highest distinction, they gave you the best champagne. Sheen later wrote, "The champagne tasted so good that night!"

C.   A titular see is a diocese that once was active but now is dormant. If someone is given a titular see, no administrative duties go along with this honorary position.

✞ CHAPTER 1 ✞

St. Thérèse the Little Flower:
The saint for troubled times

I am sure you will agree with me that we are living in troubled times. Ever since we Americans split the atom, the whole world has been split. Disturbances occur all over the world. As one Irish poet put it:

"The good lack all conviction while the worst are filled with passionate intensity."[1]

How are we going to live in these troubled times? There is really only one answer: *We have to become saints.*

When we hear that word, "saints," we generally think of canonized saints and to think of becoming like them seems almost impossible. Now some saints indeed did give us impossible things to do. We can't be like Simon Stylites^A and live on the top of a column for 20 years and

---

1 William Butler Yeats.

have food brought up to us. We can't be like St. Bernard who had 12 steps to perfect humility (I am sure that just as soon as you reach the twelfth step of humility, you will be *very* proud you are humble). Nor can we go through all of those palaces St. Teresa the Great recommended. So here we have the dilemma that *we have to become saints to be happy*, and yet how do we become one?

The Church has given us a saint for our times, and that is this young nun, St. Thérèse of Lisieux. She gave us a way to become saints that, first of all, is very simple.

Once, in a conversation with Pope John XXIII, he said to me, "You know, I always try to avoid the complicated things of life. I want everything to be simple." And St. Thérèse wanted everything to be simple. So she really had two rules. One was never to seek the satisfaction of the self, and secondly, to do everything, to bear everything out of love for our Lord.

Now you, for example, have a certain station in life. It may be on a farm, it may be in a sick bed, it may be in an office, it may be in a home. It makes no difference how humble the work is. The method of the Little Flower was to integrate sanctity with what we were doing so that there is really no one form of life that is higher than another.

For example, you may think that just simply because I appear before the public so often and talk about holy things that, therefore, I must be more holy than you! Now that is not true. There may be some old lady reading this who does not understand some big word I use but is a thousand times closer to the Good Lord than I am simply because she followed this rule of relating every single detail of life to our Blessed Lord. She integrated her life to our Lord.

That's just exactly, for example, like pouring a drop of water into wine:[B] The two become whole. Or it's like dipping an iron into fire. The iron becomes fused.

And so St. Thérèse recommended we take any action — study, work, rest, leisure (it makes no difference which) — and relate it to our Blessed Lord.

Now let me give you an example out of her life.

One of the nuns in the convent was old Sr. Peter. She was in her eighties. She was arthritic. She was cross. Nuns can be cross. So can priests be cross, God forbid! But Sr. Peter was cross, and she was in great pain, and she always had to go to the refectory about 10 minutes before the other Sisters because it took her so long to walk on account of her arthritis. Then she had to be aided as she walked, had to sit down in a chair in a special way, and had to have the bread broken for her in the bowl, always in a special way, for she had done it that way for 50 years.

Well, every other Sister found it very hard to take care of Sr. Peter, but St. Thérèse said, "I am going to do this." One day Sr. Peter said to her, "You're too young! You're a young novice. You don't know how to do anything! I think maybe you want to kill me, the way you are treating me!" And St. Thérèse would just smile back at her.

One day while she was going into the refectory with Sr. Peter, Thérèse heard music, and before her eyes, she saw a great ballroom. Sweet music was being played, dancing was on the floor, and she heard small talk that went with that kind of entertainment. For the moment, she said she was transported to the joy of this scene. Then she looked down at Sr. Peter, and she said, "For all the happiness and joyful music of the world, I would never give up Sr. Peter." And then Sr. Peter began to love her, and, of course, she always loved Sr. Peter.

Think of how many circumstances we all have in life where we have to take care of people, who perhaps are like Sr. Peter. And Thérèse made herself a saint just simply by taking care of someone who was a little cross.

Secondly, we are to see that in every sickness there is a chance to offer our sufferings up in union with our Blessed Lord. Sickness detaches us from the world. After all, I think the hand of Christ is in the "glove" of every sick person, and all we ever see is the glove. But inside is the Hand of Christ Who gave us that suffering.

So coming back now to the point, I say to live in these troubled days, we have to become saints. A saint is one who makes Christ lovable. That's the definition of a saint.

I have a friend who spent 14 years in a communist prison undergoing all kinds of torture.

When he got out of prison, he saw a little boy in the street and said to him, "Do you believe in Jesus Christ?"

The little boy said, "No, I don't."

"Well, why don't you?"

"Well," he said to my friend, "you believe Christ is God, don't you?"

"Yes."

"Well," said the little boy, "God can do many things. God made elephants, and big elephants made little elephants. God made roses, and big roses made little roses. God made monkeys. Big monkeys made little monkeys. And I think that if Jesus is God, He ought to be able to make other Jesuses. And I've never seen another Jesus. My father is an alcoholic. My mother takes in washing. She has no time for me. Nobody's ever done a good thing to me in my life. So I don't believe Jesus is God because I've never met another Jesus."

Now maybe this is what we are all supposed to be and what the Little Flower intended we should be: Little Jesuses, undergoing our passions, spreading good will and kindness just as He did. Never think you are too old. Remember, St. Thérèse died at 24. Just think of it. When many of our young people today have hardly reached the state of maturity, she was already a saint.

I just want to give you the simple lesson, and it is this: It does not require much time to make us saints, it requires only much love.

◈

Notes

A. Syrian saint, 390–459, feast day January 5.

B. At the offertory during the Mass, a drop of water is poured into the chalice of wine.

✂ CHAPTER 2 ✂

St. Thérèse and real saints
(and how you can be one, too)

Let me begin with a big word that you will have to
remember even if you forget everything else in this chapter.
It is "hagiography." Isn't that interesting? Now you've never
known a sermon on hagiography, have you?

For those of you who have forgotten your Greek, I
am going to tell you what that means. *Hagios* means "holy"
in Greek. *Graphein* means "to write." So, hagiography is the
story of the lives of saints. Now you are asking why didn't
I say that at the beginning? But no, it is necessary to talk
about that because I am telling you about the Little Flower.
So let me put her life in relationship to the lives of other
saints.

Now there are two ways of writing the lives of saints.
One is to write the life of the saint in such a way that there
is nothing bad, nothing imperfect in the life, and that is a
very common way of writing the lives of saints.

43

Take, for example, St. Aloysius. Do you know what the hagiographers say about St. Aloysius? They say that he never looked into the face of his mother. And do you think that makes him a saint? But they thought they should say that to make him sound holy.

Take, for example, St. Thomas Aquinas, one of the most learned men that ever lived. St. Thomas Aquinas loved herring, and when he went into a new monastery, one of the first things that he would ask for was herring. Do you think you can find a life of St. Thomas Aquinas in which any hagiographer says he loved herring? Saints aren't supposed to love herring.

Then St. Bernard. They said St. Bernard was so prayerful that he did not know the color of the ceiling in the monastery chapel. Now does that prove he prayed so much that he never looked up at the ceiling? You see the exaggerations there are in the lives of saints?

One of the stories of St. Bernard I like is that he was out horseback riding with a friend of his, and the friend said to him, "I never have a distraction during prayer."

St. Bernard said, "I have many."

And St. Bernard then said, "Very well, you get off your horse, and if you can say the Our Father without a single distraction, I will give you my horse."

So this friend of his got off his horse, started the Our Father, got up to the words, "Give us this day our…," and he said to Bernard, "Can I have the saddle, too?"

Now you see, doesn't that make St. Bernard much more interesting than to say he didn't know the color of the ceiling of his chapel? So there is one kind of lives of saints which make them so perfect (though their lives were not that perfect, but they are written that way). They are written to be so perfect that we cannot imitate them, we ordinary people.

There is another way of writing the lives of saints, which is the modern way. And if they could never find anything bad in the first group of hagiographers, in the second group you can't find anything good in the saints! They psychologically analyze them and if, for example, the saints practiced many mortifications, they were thought to be abnormal. If they were too prayerful, they were thought to be unconcerned with the world. So some lives have been written, even of our Little Flower, in which there is a demeaning of her sanctity. Now she can escape both of these charges because she wrote her own life.

That's the way to tell the truth. So if any of you ever intend to be saints, start writing your own life now. That's what she did. There are not many saints who did. St. Augustine did. Of course he had a lot to tell because he was the "hippie" of his day and a very wild young man. So his story is indeed an interesting one, though do you know that when you read the life of St. Augustine, you would think that the only bad thing he ever did in his life was to steal pears? He tells about that in the first chapter, and he makes the stealing of pears stand for all the wicked things that he did during his life.

Few saints have written their lives. I don't think we could say that St. Teresa wrote her life (I do not mean the Little Flower. I mean St. Teresa of Avila, Spain), though she wrote volumes about sanctity. And also St. John of the Cross. Wouldn't you think that there would be some pride in writing your life if you were a saint? Now I am going to prove you are all saints, though you haven't written your life. But you are saints.

St. Thérèse wrote her life in obedience because she was a good religious. In a conversation one night in the convent someone suggested that it would be interesting to have Sr. Thérèse write the story of her girlhood. She didn't think it was very interesting, but the Mother Superior ordered her to write her life.

Now this is the beginning of her life which I am going to share with you. She is addressing it, you see, to the Mother Superior of the convent. So when you write your life, you must address it to somebody else, otherwise you would be very proud and vain if you said, "I want to tell everybody how holy I am."

> Dearest Mother, it is to you, who are my mother
> twice over, that I am going to tell the history of
> my soul. When you first asked me to do it, I
> was frightened. It looked as if I was wasting my
> spiritual energies on introspection. But since
> then our Lord has made it clear to me that all
> He wanted of me was plain obedience. And in

any case, I shall be doing only what will be my
task in eternity, telling over and over again the
story of God's mercies to me.

That was, incidentally, the reason that St. Augustine
wrote his *Confessions*, in order to explain the mercies of
God. But he had more need of the mercies of God than
St. Thérèse.

Now continuing:

Before taking up my pen, I knelt down before
Our Lady's statue, the one which has so often
assured us that the Queen of Heaven looks on
our family of nuns with special favor. My prayer
was that she should guide my hand and never let
me write a single line which wasn't as she
wanted it to be. After that I opened the gospels
at random and the words my eyes fell on were
these [she is quoting here the Gospel of St.
Mark]:

"Then He went up on the mountain-side and
called to Him those whom it pleased Him to
call. And these came to Him."[1]

There it all was. The mystery of my life, my
vocation, above all, the special claims that Jesus
makes on my soul. He does not call the people
who are worthy of it. No, just the people it

---

1 Mark 3:13

pleases Him to call. As St. Paul says, "God shows pity on those He pities, mercy where I am merciful."[2] And I had always wondered why it was that God has His preferences instead of giving each soul an equal degree of grace. Why does He shower extraordinary favors on the saints who at one time had been His enemies? People like St. Paul and St. Augustine, compelling them to accept the graces He sends them.

And then she goes on to say...

I have really more mercies than any other saint because God prevented me from sinning. Otherwise I would have been a great sinner. So the story of my life is the story of God's mercies.

So in this simple little book (which you must read again because I know that you all have read it once, the life of the Little Flower), she spends a great deal of time on her youth. But what comes out in every single chapter is her desire to be perfect.

There is a danger in writing your own life. The danger is if one is depending on oneself, one may fall into errors of theology and Scripture and the like. Do you know how she kept straight in her life and why anyone can follow her book as a spiritual guide? She had two great protections: On the one side was the *Imitation of Christ* by

---

2 Cf. Rom 9:15

Thomas à Kempis (that she always kept with her because in the *Imitation of Christ*, it is always Christ who is speaking to the soul), and the other book was Scripture.

St. Thérèse was a real biblical scholar, something that we must remember to perfect our lives. *We must read Scripture.*

She has 107 quotations from the Old Testament and 250 quotations from the New Testament [in her book]. Think of that! One-hundred and seven from the Old. And she did not study Scripture as the scholar does. For example, she picked up the prophet Isaiah, and she read, she said, about 50 chapters before there came to her an inspiration that she applied to her own life. And that she would memorize.

When she was appointed sacristan, for example, she went to Scripture. She kept reading, and finally she hit on Isaiah 52:11:

> Away from Babylon [Babylon was the wicked city]; come out, come out, touch nothing unclean. Come out from Babylon, keep yourselves pure, you who carry the vessels of the Lord.

See how she applied that to herself and likewise in many other instances of Scripture. So her life, therefore, became a very sound guide for perfection.

Now this is the idea that I want to leave with you.

You see, we grow physically. There are young people who are growing physically. We have another life in us besides the physical which is our spiritual life. That should never grow old. St. Paul tells us that as the body declines, the spirit gets younger. No old people enter the Kingdom of Heaven. Don't let that frighten you, anyone who's over 39! But it is a fact. Our Lord said that unless you become as little children, you cannot enter the Kingdom of Heaven.

You see, we have two ways of measuring age, distance from the source of life. For example, a child of ten is older than a child of six because the ten year old is four years more distant from the source of life, his parents. But we have another source of life than our parents, namely God. Therefore, the closer that we get to God, the younger we become. Now some of you people who think you're old are already living in nurseries, really, because you are already close to God. Therefore, there was no reason for her to live beyond the age of 24. She reached her birthday.

Have you ever noticed that the Church never celebrates a birthday the same as the world? You celebrate a birthday on which you were born from your parents. But the Church celebrates the birthdays on which we die. We call it *natalitia*, birthday. We get younger and younger and younger because we get back to the source of life, which is our God.

Now applying this to ourselves ... her life is a struggle for perfection. Most of us settle down to mediocrity. We level off, particularly about middle age. We cannot do that spiritually. We *have* to grow, we *have* to become younger.

We *have* to become closer to God. It makes no difference what happens to the body then. It's the spirit that must grow, and it doesn't make any difference how many sins you've had in your life, you still must strive for perfection.

Now let me give you some courage along those lines. See, the Little Flower attained perfection when she was very young, and she had the absolute certitude that she was going to Heaven. We'll talk about that later, and why, therefore, she had no fear of death. But coming to the idea that you, too, must strive for perfection, not just go on doing the same things every day but do them with greater love, greater intensity, bearing things in union with the sufferings of our Blessed Lord, loving your neighbor more, speaking less uncharitably of neighbors, starting now!

I am going to give you the way sacred Scripture writes the lives of saints. I told you at the beginning of how some hagiographers praise the saints and never say they did anything bad. Others only point out the bad things and never say the good things. Now let's open Scripture at the eleventh chapter of the Letter to the Hebrews. In the epistle to the Hebrews, the eleventh chapter, we have the saints of the Old Testament. And I want you to derive courage from this chapter and to see that you, too, can strive for perfection as the Little Flower did. Here we come to Noah and Abraham:

> By faith Noah, divinely warned about the
> unseen future, took good heed and built an ark
> to save his household. Through his faith he put

the whole world in the wrong...[3]

This is something very good said about Noah. Do you find a word in here about the fact that Noah once got drunk? No, but he did, after the Flood.[4] He strove for perfection and so he gets recorded now in the New Testament as a man of great faith. So alcoholics can start again. Noah did.

Now we come to Abraham. He is praised 11 times in this chapter for his faith.

> By faith Abraham obeyed the call to go out to
> a land destined for himself and his heirs, and
> left home without knowing where he would go.
> By faith he settled as an alien in the land
> promised him, living in tents...[5]

If you want to find out this full story of Abraham, you go back to the Old Testament, and you find out that he lied twice.[6] He had a very beautiful wife, and while he was journeying through the lands, all the pagan people tried to get hold of his wife. And he lied about her twice. Do you find that in the New Testament? No! He became perfect,

---

3 Here Sheen quotes Heb 11:7. Other translations read, "By faith Noah, being warned by God concerning events as yet unseen, took heed and constructed an ark for the saving of his household; by this he condemned the world ..." and "By faith Noe, having received an answer concerning those things which as yet were not seen, moved with fear, framed the ark for the saving of his house, by the which he condemned the world ..."
4 Cf. Gen 9:20-21
5 Heb 11:8-9
6 Cf. Gen 12:9-20

but he was not perfect at the beginning.

Then we go on to Jacob, and Jacob is now praised for his faith:

> By faith Isaac blessed Jacob and Esau and spoke of things to come. By faith Jacob, as he was dying, blessed each of Joseph's sons and worshipped God...[7]

When you go back in the Old Testament what do you find out about Jacob? He was a crook! He was a mafioso! He was a deceiver! He was a knave! But he became a saint! See, Scripture does not leave out the bad things of the saints. This is the real life of saints here.

And then we go from Abraham and Isaac and Jacob on to Moses. And Moses is praised for his sanctity. Did you know that Moses killed a man? He did![8] But he became a saint. He became perfect, so perfect that he is called "God's friend."[9] Think of that! God's friend!

I once talked in a large prison where there were 1,979 inmates. I can't tell you how consoled some of those men were when I told them that Moses once committed murder, too. Immediately they said, "Well, there is a chance for me."

So if you ever want, therefore, to find hope in the

---

7 Heb 11:21
8 Cf. Ex 2:11-12
9 Cf. Ex 33:11

lives of the saints, go to the epistle of the Hebrews, where you find a list of all of these saints. Go back and see their failures and then, eventually, how they overcame them.

Coming back to the life of the Little Flower, the one thing that interested her was being perfect, not like everyone else. When she was a little girl, very small, her older sister Léonie was getting too big to play with dolls. One day when Thérèse and her other sister Céline were seated on the lawn, Léonie came out with a big basket filled with small dolls with strips of material and small pieces of lace. And when Léonie laid the basket down, she took a big doll, and she put it on top of the basket, and she said, "Alright, sisters, now choose what you want."

Thérèse reached out and said, "I'll take everything."

And she said, "This became the rule of my life. I wanted everything. I wanted to be perfect. I wanted to be God's."

You know the only reason we are unhappy, my good people, is because we are not striving enough to be holy as she was, wanting everything. We are like trapeze artists. We just let go of one trapeze, and we're still in mid-air, and we haven't caught hold of the other ... and we're not sure we will. But when there is a resolute will to *do* everything and *bear* everything for God's sake, then life becomes happy on the inside.

So this is our first lesson about the Little Flower and a lesson of hope for you. May we never give up hope. You are much better than you think you are. All of you. You wouldn't be reading this otherwise. First of all, you are kind, otherwise you wouldn't have bought this book! Second, you are patient, otherwise you wouldn't have stayed with me this far. Third, you are charitable. Fourth, you have a lot of fortitude because you continue along with me. And so I might go on with all the other virtues.

Now you've got a good start for perfecting your life, so pray now to the Little Flower to not be ordinary. You know, what is killing the world today is ordinariness. Flatness. Dullness. Want of fire. We can't be happy unless we are in love, and when we have perfect love, which is the love of God, then we are supremely happy. You already have this love in great measure.

So then picture St. Thérèse again on her lawn reaching out for the basket of dolls saying, "I want everything." And *you* say you want everything. You want perfect life. That's what you want, not for a few more years. You want truth, not just the truths of literature to the exclusion of science. You want love, not a love that knows satiety or fed-up-ness. You want perfect life and perfect truth and perfect love, and that's God.

The way of St. Thérèse is easy. It's living the life that you are living now, only making it holy. You sacramentalize it.

For example, take the water in the baptismal font. See how the Church uses that as a symbol for cleaning the soul? The bread is matter that's used to communicate to you the divine life in the Eucharist, and oil is for healing in the Sacrament of the Sick. So your housework, your office work, whatever you happen to do, that's where you start to be a saint. There. What the Little Flower gives us is this supreme lesson in contrast with the past. She's very modern. There is no need of anyone wearing a hair shirt. Our neighbors are hair shirts! Life is a hair shirt! We have to put up with it.

So if you want to know where you start to be a saint, start right where you are now. Only, *want* to be perfect, saying to God, "I want everything. I want *You*." That's love. That's happiness.

☙ CHAPTER 3 ❧

St. Thérèse and the virtues of faith, hope, and perseverance

My dear friends, I know that many of you have been praying for some special favor for a long time, and you probably are disappointed in the good Lord. I am immediately reminded of a girl who came to me at the end of a church service in New York, and she asked me if I would help get her brother into the United States from the Philippine Islands.

She said, "I used to be a Catholic, but I'm not a Catholic anymore, and I do not want you to mention anything about the Church to me. I just want to talk about my brother."

I said, "Alright, you come to see me tomorrow."

When she came, I took her into the chapel. I didn't talk about her brother, and I said, "Dear Lord, here is a girl who is mad at You. She asked You for a favor, and You did not give it to her. So, because she does not like the Captain of the ship, she is going to jump overboard."

I let her go, and I told her to come back the next day. When she came back, I said, "Come in to confession."

She went to confession! Now, she was trying to put me off, you see, but I knew really she wanted to come back, so you must not despair now of your prayers.

I'm going to tell you about the Little Flower in relationship to love's delays. Love is not immediate. Scripture, therefore, often tells us to "wait on the Lord."[1] Wait. For example, in the prophet Isaiah, God speaks in the 30th chapter, the 18th verse.

> The Lord is waiting to show you His favor. He yearns to have pity on you, and happy are all who wait for Him.

The Little Flower at one time did not want to wait on Him. When she was fourteen-and-a-half years of age, she wanted to enter the monastery at Carmel...not to enter at fourteen-and-a-half, but enter at 15. She went to her father for whom she had the deepest affection, and he said, "What is it, little princess, that you want?"

She said, "I want to enter Carmel at the age of 15."

---

1 For example, Ps 27:14; 37:7, 34; 62:5; Prov 20:22; Is 40:31; Lam 3:26; Micah 7:7; Rom 8:24-25; etc.

They walked up and down the garden, and he picked up a flower, and not just the flower, but even the roots came up. So he said to her, "Yes, you may enter." And he gave her the flower, which later on she kept pressed in her copy of the book, *The Imitation of Christ*.

She said, "The very fact that the roots were there indicated to me that I was to have roots somewhere else than in my home."

She was very happy that she had received her father's consent, but still, not wanting to wait too long, she went to her uncle [and legal guardian Isidore Guérin, a local pharmacist and editor of a conservative Catholic newspaper].

And he said, "No, this is ridiculous, a girl of 15 entering Carmel!"

She then went to her pastor, and he said no. She went to the Mother Superior of the Carmel monastery. Mother Superior said, "No, you are too young."

She went to the vicar general of the diocese, and the vicar general said, "No, you must wait until you are 21."

Then she went to the bishop, and as she was ushered into the bishop, the secretary said, "Now no diamonds," meaning do not shed any tears, but there were a lot of diamonds just the same. She said she saw all the pictures of the bishops of the diocese in the big hall as she went in. She felt so very small in the presence of those great paintings, and she asked the bishop, and he said, no, she was too young.

"Well, is there any recourse?"

"Yes," he said, "you can ask the Holy Father."

So she went to Rome with her father. Now the Pontiff in those days was one of the greatest of all of the pontiffs of the Church. It was the great Leo XIII, a very formal and very learned man.

When the party from Lisieux came into the audience room, the pastor turned to them all and said, "Now remember, no one is to speak."

And her sister Céline said, "You talk." So Thérèse knelt down before the Holy Father who was seated in a white chair and she said "Your Holiness, inasmuch as this is your Jubilee Year, would you allow me to enter Carmel at the age of 15?"

With that the pastor said, "Your Holiness, she is only a child, and the superiors are looking into this matter."

But still the Little Flower did not give up.

She said, "But Holy Father, you can do anything. Just tell me I can enter, then I can enter."

And he said, "If it is the will of God, you will enter Carmel."

Then she started to speak again, and Pope Leo put his finger on her lips, and one of the papal guards touched her on the shoulder. That was the saddest day of her life.

Now she had to learn the lesson of love's delays. How did she take it? Some people in disappointment leave the Church. Let me share a paragraph with you from her own autobiography. She wrote:

> For some time I have indulged the fancy of offering myself up to the Child Jesus as a plaything for Him to do with what He liked with me. I don't mean an expensive plaything. Give a child an expensive toy, and he will sit looking at it, afraid to touch it. But a toy of no value, a ball, say, is all at His disposal. He can throw it on the ground, kick it about, make a hole in it, leave it in a corner or press it to his heart, however he feels about it.
>
> In the same way, I wanted our Lord to do exactly what He liked with me, and here in Rome, He has taken me at my word. In Rome, the Child Jesus made a hole in the ball to see what was on the inside of it. Then satisfied with that, He threw the ball away and went to sleep. Who is to tell us what the Child was dreaming about while the ball lay there neglected? Perhaps He dreamed that He was still playing with it, first dropping it and then picking it up. Letting it roll a long way and then pressing it to His Heart to make sure that it never slipped from

His Hand. Yes, He can do with it what He likes.
But you see, Reverend Mother, it's a depressing
sensation to feel that you are like that ball that
has been thrown aside.

So the Little Flower had what she said was the
greatest disappointment of her life, not to enter Carmel at
15. But she did! First, she had to learn the lesson of defeat
as she learned it then in Rome.

You see, there are two philosophies of life. One is the
pagan philosophy: First the feast, then the headache. The
other is the Christian philosophy of life: First the fast, then
the feast. Our law is first Good Friday, then Easter Sunday.
First the cross, then the empty tomb. So she is now having
her cross. Just contrast, for example, the sorrow that this
little girl of fourteen-and-a-half had in that visit to Rome
in contrast with the glorification that we are now giving
her on this centenary of her birth.[A]

In the meantime there was this delay of God's
love. Now let me explain that to you at greater length,
particularly from Scripture. Think of how God tested
Noah, for example. Noah lived in the desert, and He told
Noah to build an ark. Can you imagine the sarcasm, the
sneers that poor Noah must have had simply because he
obeyed God? And here he is building this ark in a desert!
Nothing to float on! But he just took God's word for it
that it would come true. This was love's delay.

Take Abraham. God said to Abraham, "You will have
children as numerous as the sands of the sea and as the stars

of the heavens."[2] That was God's promise. But when he is 98 years old and Sarah is 80, he doesn't have a son. Both of them are past the age of conceiving, but God had told him that he would have progeny as numerous as the stars. There was this long delay until it passed almost into the realm of the impossible. And then he had a son, Isaac.

Then we come to the New Testament. A classic example is the story of Lazarus. Our Blessed Lord was beyond the Jordan River with His disciples, and news came to Him that Lazarus was dead. Now Lazarus was His friend. He had been there many times at his home [the one he shared with his sisters Martha and Mary], and He owed him, from a human point of view, some obligation and consideration.

And the apostles said, "Will you go?"

And our Lord said, "No, I will not go."

So He waited two days. Oh, yes, the message that came at first was that Lazarus was sick. Now even if the story had stopped there, wouldn't you say, well what love did our Lord have for Lazarus? Here's His best friend sick, and He does not go near him? And the Lord stayed two days more, and news came that Lazarus was dead.

Thomas, always sad, downhearted, expecting rain the day of the picnic, said, "Let's go and die with him."

---

2 Gen 22:26

And our Lord said, "No, I am glad this has happened. I am glad because it will show forth the power of God."

Then it took two days' journey to get to Bethany where Lazarus was buried. There was not a great deal of faith on Martha's part when our Lord came.

And she said "Well, Lord if You had been here, he would not have died."

And He said, "Where is he buried?"

And they said, "It is no use now. He stinks already."[3]

Now suppose the story stopped here? Would we not complain against God's mercy and love? And yet in the end, God raised Lazarus from the dead. Did you ever notice in Scripture that no dead person ever remained dead in the presence of our Lord? For example, the daughter of Jairus,[4] the son of the widow of Naim,[5] and Lazarus. In the presence of death there is Life who is Christ Himself. Here again was love's delay.

And then one other instance of love's delay in the New Testament was the Syrophoenician woman. Now this was not a Jewish woman. She lived in the pagan part of the land in which our Lord lived. She had a daughter who was terribly troubled by a demon. She cried out, "Lord, Son of David, have pity on me!"

---

3 Cf. John 11:1-44
4 Cf. Mark 5:21-43
5 Cf. Luke 7:11-17

✖ Archbishop Sheen preaches the novena of talks that form the basis for this book at Whitefriars Church, Dublin. The prelate in the background is Archbishop Gaetano Alibrandi, who served as papal nuncio to Ireland for 20 years.

St. Thérèse in July 1876 at three-years-old. Her mother later wrote she was on the verge of tears here because she did not want her picture taken.

Thérèse, on the right at age 8, with her sister Céline, 12. Notice Thérèse's jump rope.

❧ Thérèse's parents, Louis and Zélie (née Guérin) Martin. Pope John Paul II declared both "venerable" on March 26, 1994.

❧ St. Thérèse at age 13, the year she had her Christmas conversion.

❧ Thérèse at 15-years-old, taken several days before her entrance into the Carmel convent at Lisieux.

ᴥ St. Thérèse poses in her novice's habit shortly after she received it on January 10, 1889.

St. Thérèse at recreation (date uncertain). Notice the serene quality of her face.

The Little Flower with her fellow nuns in 1894 during a time of meditation in the convent's grotto.

✎ Seen here in the Spring of 1895, St. Thérèse portrays her heroine St. Joan of Arc as a prisoner (notice the chain). For the other nuns' amusement, Thérèse produced a play based on the martyr's life in which she played the lead.

✎ In another pose as St. Joan (here showing Joan's vision of St. Margaret).

The Little Flower, standing to the right of center tree in July 1896 during the community haying.

St. Thérèse poses as a sacristan here with her sisters and cousin in November 1896.

As with many photos of St. Thérèse, her sister Céline took this July 1896 picture. She told Thérèse to affect the same facial expression she had "in the picture … when she was eight."

A year later, July 7, 1897, it was evident Thérèse would soon die. This photo was made as a keepsake for the other nuns. Notice the Little Flower holds prayer cards of the Child Jesus and the Holy Face (she was officially known as St. Thérèse of the Child Jesus and the Holy Face).

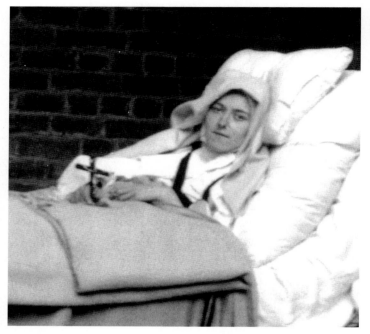

❧ Here the sisters have set up a bed for St. Thérèse in the cloister, enabling her to enjoy some fresh air on a late August day in 1897. This photo was the last taken of her alive.

❦ October 1, 1897, St. Thérèse is seen here one day after her death looking beautiful and serene. Taken by Céline in the infirmary.

❧ Archbishop Sheen with Fr. Andrew Apostoli, CFR. The two met while Apostoli was a seminarian, and Sheen later ordained Apostoli to the priesthood in 1967. This picture was taken after Sheen gave a talk to the cadets at West Point ca. 1974-75. Fr. Andrew went backstage to say hello to the archbishop, and the two friends took this photo together.

❧ Fr. Linus Ryan, O. Carm., greets the archbishop at Dublin's airport as he arrives to preach the talks that became this book. Sheen made four trips to Dublin at Fr. Ryan's invitation.

✣ Sheen as a young priest at the University of Louvain in Belgium during the 1920s.

✣ Circa the mid-1930s after Pope Pius XI had made him a monsignor. Sheen knew Pius, who once gave him a silver crucifix inlaid with ebony.

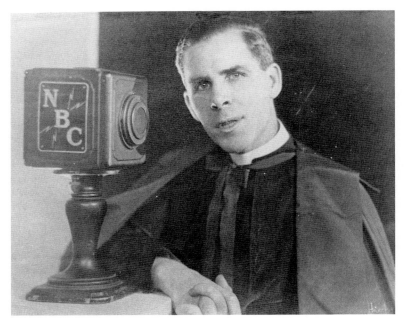

❧ Msgr. Sheen poses with an NBC radio microphone ca. the mid-1930s. Until 1951, a generation of people associated Sheen with the radio, a medium that helped him garner a weekly audience of four million and made him one of America's best known Catholic priests.

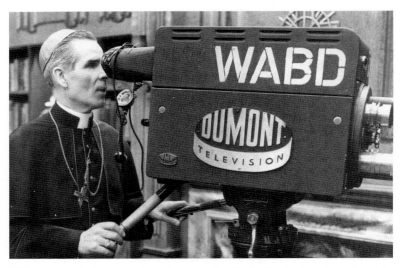

❧ May 1952, the archbishop observes what life is like on the other side of the camera.

❧ Archbishop Sheen shows some of the passion for which he was famous.

❧ Sheen during the first broadcast of "Life is Worth Living" in 1951. Notice the initials "JMJ" (Jesus, Mary, Joseph), which were on top of everything he wrote.

❧ Bishop Sheen helps a young fan model some of the trappings of his episcopal office ca. 1955.

❧ Msgr. Sheen, April 1947, greeting well-wishers at the groundbreaking for Bl. Martin de Porres Hospital in Mobile, AL, which was specifically built to serve African Americans in the then-segregated South. Along with Archbishop T.J. Toolen of Mobile-Birmingham (the same bishop who invited Mother Angelica to Alabama), he helped raise $225,000 for the project ($1,820,525 in today's dollars), with donations coming from every state in the Union. Sheen's involvement with this project shows the commitment he had to civil rights, social justice, and Catholic outreach to black Americans. With the advent of civil rights, the hospital closed, and the facility is now the Allen Memorial nursing home.

Archbishop Sheen in 1959, standing in the same spot on the Sea of Galilee where Jesus told Peter, "Feed my lambs."

The archbishop praying before the Blessed Sacrament, something he did for an hour each day. He credited the strength of his ministry to this practice.

❧ Bishop Sheen officiating at the wedding between Archduke Rudolph Habsburg of Austria and Countess Xenia Tschernyschev-Besobrasow, June 22, 1953, at Our Lady of Mt. Carmel Church, Tuxedo Park, NY.

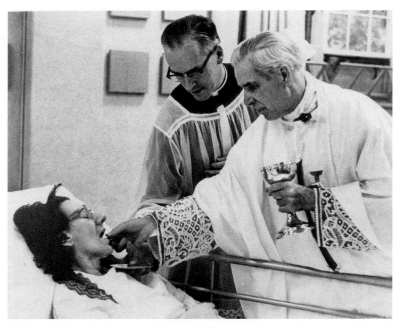

❧ Visiting the sick while bishop of Rochester (ca. 1966-69).

✺ Archbishop Sheen distributes Communion at the Marian shrine in Lourdes, France, during one of roughly 30 visits he made there.

✺ Sheen shakes hands with a Monroe County, NY, inmate after blessing him on Christmas Day, 1966, shortly after his installation as bishop of Rochester. It was believed to be the first visit by a local bishop to an area prison.

🔊 Top to Bottom: The Servant of God Fulton Sheen with four popes, three of whom he knew well and with whom he was friends: the Servant of God Pius XII (June 1957), Bl. John XXIII (ca. 1962), the Servant of God Paul VI (ca. 1974), and the Servant of God John Paul II (New York's Cathedral of St. Patrick, October 2, 1979). In the photo with John Paul II, the pontiff is telling the archbishop, "You have written and spoken well of the Lord Jesus. You are a loyal son of the Church."

But Jesus tested the faith of this woman because "He gave her no word of response."

Even Jesus' disciples added to love's delay. They came up to the Lord, not to entreat Him to help the woman, but to complain, "Get rid of her! She keeps shouting after us!"

Jesus does not send her away, but again tests her trust by seeming to exclude her as a Gentile woman, "My mission is only to the lost sheep of the House of Israel." But even this hurdle does not break the woman's confidence, for she falls at the feet of Jesus with a heartfelt plea, "Help me, Lord!"

Our Lord now seemingly says something hard, so we have to be persistent in our love even when there is a delay. He said, "It is not fitting to take the bread of the children and throw it to dogs." The bread of the children – that would be the bread for the Jews. What did the Jews call the pagans? Dogs. So our Lord said it is not fitting to take the bread that is reserved for the Jews and give it to the pagans.

But she answers Him, saying, "But even the dogs eat the crumbs that fall from the master's table."

And our Lord answered, "I have not seen such faith in all of Israel," and then He healed her daughter.[6]

Now there may be in this incident of love's delay a

---

6 Cf. Matt 15:21-28

deeper mystery still. Our Blessed Lord was trying to teach His apostles to love all peoples. The Jews in those times said you could thank God you were not born a dog ... or a Gentile. Our Lord was trying to teach His apostles that they had to love everyone in the world, even Gentiles.

Now here comes a Gentile woman. The apostles were ready to chase her away. I think that our Blessed Lord really winked at that woman in order to draw her out saying, "It is not fitting to take the bread of children and throw it to the dogs." I don't believe He was talking to her as much as He was talking to the apostles to remind them they were to love everyone.

But to keep up the point. Here all through Scripture is the delay of love. If you start with a great success you may be like a skyrocket. Go up with a lot of fire and noise and come down like a stick. Some of the hardest and cruelest words in sacred Scripture are, "You have already had your reward."[7] You wanted something? You got it. That's all you'll ever have. So the Lord sometimes does not give us all that we want. But even when we do not receive it, we can find a divine answer as she did.

A little girl shortly before Christmas time had told her father she wanted a thousand dolls for Christmas. And on Christmas day, the father who was an unbeliever said to his daughter, "Well, God didn't answer your prayers did He?

---

7 Cf. Matt 6:2, 5, 16

She said, "Oh yes, He did! God said no."

God sometimes does say no in love's delays.

Coming back now to the Little Flower, this is one of the dark moments of her life. She was asked — I think it was by the vicar general of the diocese — how long have you wanted to be a nun? She said, "All my life."

Even though it was only fourteen-and-a-half years, it is difficult for us to put ourselves in a position of a young girl with such love of the solitary contemplative life and being frustrated by the Pontiff himself! Other people would leave the Church. What does she do? She said, "Well, I'm delighting the Lord anyway. I'm just the ball, and He doesn't want to play with it. He's not amused with it. He just wants to put a hole in it, that's all. Leave it in the corner." So she was content to be in the corner.

Now then, if you are praying for certain favors, be prepared for love's delay, but keep on praying. Do not give up. There, for example, are some beautiful words of our Blessed Lord from the Gospel of Luke on praying. Our Lord tells the story of a crotchety, cranky old judge. Our Lord almost seems to compare Himself to that judge! And this is the story He tells. He spoke to them a parable to show they should keep on praying. Never lose heart. After all, isn't that what courtship is? A young woman plays hard to get in order to draw out love. So does God sometimes play hard to get.

There was once a judge who cared nothing for

God or man. In the same town there was a widow who constantly came before him demanding justice against her opponent. Now can't you get this picture, in a small village, of a poor old woman going to this judge *day after day* until the judge is almost driven crazy by her. And then our Lord continues. "For a long time He refused. But in the end, he said to himself, 'True, I care nothing for God or man. But this widow is such a nuisance that I will give her justice before she wears me out with her persistence.'"

And the Lord said, "Do you hear what the unjust judge says? And will not God vindicate His chosen ones who cry out to Him day and night while He patiently listens to them? I tell you He will vindicate them soon enough. When the Son of Man comes, however, do you think He will find faith on earth?"[8]

So never give up your prayer, because the petition that you seek is distinct from the prayer itself. All prayer is dependence. Prayer is love. And you will find that as you love more you will be seeking less and less material favors. Maybe God is answering our prayers without our knowing it very often. In the divine intent, the day that Pope Leo put his finger over the lips of that fourteen-and-a-half year old girl, God had already decided that she was going to enter Carmel. And I am sure that when Pope Leo went to Heaven, the one thing that he was most sorry for in his whole life was that he told that little girl to keep still. Here we are praying to the Little Flower and not to Leo XIII. What a lesson that is! I am sure few readers have said

---

8 Luke 18:2-8

a prayer to Leo XIII, as great as he was, and he controlled the life of the Little Flower. You see, everything changes in the mind of God.

That is often why, when I go out to dinner in rectories and religious communities and the like, I always try to see the cooks. And I say to them, "You're working in the kitchen over a hot stove, and you're serving us who are seated here at table in comfort. But everything's going to be changed. This is evidenced in the parable of Lazarus the poor man, and the rich man who gave him nothing. In heaven, all you cooks and you who serve tables are going to sit at table in heaven, and we bishops are going to cook for you! Now, I do my own cooking, but let me tell you, I'm a terrible cook. But when we get to Heaven, you needn't worry about the cooking because with the Beatific Vision comes the power of cooking, so you'll be treated very well. But everything will be turned upside down."

On this day Leo XIII and a fourteen–and–a–half year old girl have reversed their positions. She is there on the altar. We are reading Mass to her, not to Leo XIII. She had to suffer the great delays of God, and even our wait for heaven is a delay, and I will next tell you the Little Flower's view of death.

Notes

A.   Her birth's centenary was 1973, the year these talks were given.

❧ CHAPTER 4 ❦

St. Thérèse and the power of intercession

I am going to talk to you about death and St. Thérèse's attitude toward it, which is, I am sure, quite different from our own. We all dread it, principally because it is the last penalty of sin, our last debt that we all have to pay, but not a great debt because our Blessed Lord died for us. That we must always remember. He went through it first.

I can remember when I was a little boy, we were often given castor oil. I hated it. I hope the rising generation of boys and girls never has to take castor oil. My grandmother would give me the castor oil, but she would always take some herself first. She would taste it, and she said, "See? It's good." Well, now, I know it killed her just as it killed me, but she wanted to convince me that it wasn't bad.

That's what our Lord did when He took our death. He said, "See, I've tasted it. It's not as bad as you think." Let us put death in a real broad perspective. There are actually three wombs. One is the womb of nature by which we are born physically, the second is the womb of grace, and the third is the womb of eternity.

First, the womb of nature. Just suppose that we were all conscious in our mother's womb. Do you think we would have wanted to be born? We probably would have said, "Well, I don't know what's out there. Here I'm alive, I'm cared for. Out there is an unknown world, and I'm frightened to go into it." But when we got into it, it wasn't so bad.

Then the second birth is grace. We are only creatures by nature, and when we receive grace, we have another birth. Now we do not feel this shock so much because most of us were baptized as infants, but those who are converts and struggled for the faith will tell you that they went through labor pains of the spirit in order to be born to grace, and we have to continue that in mortification.

The third womb is death, when we are born to eternity. We shrink from entrance into eternity just the same as we would have shrunk from being born from our mother's womb into time. Because we are not quite sure of where we are going, what our destiny will be, though we have a sound belief in the future life in union with Christ. These are the three doors we have to face and open.

Now what was the attitude of the Little Flower about death? Well, she was anxious to die first of all, and she died very young. When she was sick, she asked her Reverend Mother – to whom she was subject in obedience – if the Reverend Mother would give her permission to die. The

Reverend Mother refused, so the Little Flower said, "You know, our Blessed Lord is very anxious for a bunch of grapes that's hanging in this world, and I'm that bunch of grapes."

"And our Lord is a thief," she said. Remember He called Himself a thief. Remember when He said, "I will come like a thief in the night"?[1]

So she said, "Our Blessed Lord will come and steal this bunch of grapes, and if you say, 'Thief, thief!' I will say, 'This way, this way, this way!'"

That's how she welcomed death.

One of the priests who was taking care of her at death said, "Are you resigned to dying?"

She said, "I don't need any resignation to die, I need a resignation to live." She said, "I have lived for our Lord, I want to die for Him. This is my Love, and I want to be with the Beloved."

It was that simple. What then was her judgment like? Do you think she went to purgatory? No. She said she wouldn't go to purgatory. That's confidence, isn't it? That was not pride. She said, "What is there in purgatory to burn?"

She said, "I have been a victim of Divine Love. I've

---

1 Cf. Matt 24:42-43; 1 Thes 5:1-5

burned myself out *for* Him and, therefore, there will be nothing to burn *in* me for purgatory."

She wasn't inflammable. Now not many of us would have that attitude about purgatory. Some of us would feel rather lucky to get there.

Did you ever hear the story of the monks that had to get up very early in the mornings, at three o'clock for meditation? And one of them always came down late, just in time for Mass at five o'clock but never for meditation. And the superior called him in and said, "Now tomorrow morning when the bell rings at three o'clock for meditation, I want you to think that you are in purgatory. And the flames of purgatory are enveloping you, and you immediately bound out of bed and come down to meditation."

Next morning he was late. The superior called him in and asked, "Did you do what I told you to do?"

"Yes," he said, "I did, but I *love* purgatory."

Well now, the Little Flower didn't love purgatory, and she was sure that she was not going there because purgatory would be a place where the dross is burned off as we burn dross off gold.^A And what will the judgment be like? Do not ever think the Judgment—for those of you who have the faith and are trying to love the Good Lord—do not think that it is going to be fearful, that it is only the God of justice and not the God of mercy Who is going to judge you.

I will tell you what it's like and why the Little Flower didn't feel she ever had to go to purgatory.

Just suppose I owed you some money, say $10, and I'd owed it to you for a long time. And I saw you coming down the street, and I didn't have $10. What would I do? I'd cross the street, wouldn't I, to get away from you because you'd remind me of a debt.

Now when we go before the sight of God, remember, on the one hand, we will be very conscious of our failings and our sins and our debts, and we will pull back from the presence of Christ in shame. But on the other hand, what have we lived for all our lives? We've lived for Him. That's why you come to church. That's why you go to Communion. That's why you pray, why you are patient in suffering. Your whole life is Christ-dedicated.

So, you see, you will be squeezed in between two movements. On the one hand a deep sense of unworthiness which will pull you away from the Lord, and a tremendous sense of attraction because you want Him and He wants you. And when you get caught between those two feelings, that's going to be a deep, burning sensation. That's purgatory.

How long it will last we do not know. It may be very quick. But the Little Flower, you see, never had a moment as she perfected herself when she would ever want to draw back from Christ. Hers was only attraction, and that's why she said, "I will go straight to heaven."

I hope none of you considers that as pride. I understand it solely in terms of someone who loves deeply.

Now we come to her intercessory power in heaven. And this is a point where I believe we need deep instruction, intercession. We do not mention it enough, perhaps, in our sermons and in our teaching, but intercession means pleading for others. Now let me read you some of the last words of the Little Flower about her intercession:

> Confidently I count upon not remaining inactive in heaven. My desire is to still work for the Church and for souls.

You see, she didn't think that heaven was a place of total repose. She says, "I'm going to work in heaven."

In another place she says, "Because I withdraw from the battlefield, I'm not going to be at rest."

To continue her words:

> This I shall ask of God, and I am certain that He will hear me. If I quit already the battlefield, it is not with a selfish desire of taking my rest. Suffering has long since become my heaven here below, and it is difficult to imagine how it will be possible for me to become acclimatized to a country where joy reigns unmingled with any sorrow. Jesus must need to transform my soul completely as I couldn't stand eternal bliss.

In other words, she said, "When I go to heaven, I do not lose my interest in this world, I keep it." Therefore, she became very confident that she would be our advocate and our attorney in the Kingdom of Heaven. And continuing her thought:

> Just now a few notes of distant music fall upon my ear and set me thinking that very soon I shall hear melodies beyond compare. Yet this thought cannot give me but a moment's gladness. Only one expectation makes my heart throb. It is the love that I shall receive and the love that I shall be able to give. I feel that my mission is now to begin. My mission is to make others love the good God as I love Him, to give to souls my little way. I will spend my heaven in doing good upon the earth.

"Spend my heaven in doing good upon the earth." She was on this earth, and she was not known outside of her little convent. Now she said, "I'm going to be active." Remember our Blessed Lord said, "My Father works, and so do I work."[2]

Intercession is something tremendous in theology. You know who your great intercessors are? Two. One is our Lord in heaven, as Scripture says, always making intercession for us,[3] I think, at every Mass, for example. And when I say Mass today, if we may picture—it's only a picture—but if we may depict in some way what our Lord

---

2 Cf. John 5:17
3 Cf. Rom 8:34

does at the Mass, it would be showing His scars to His heavenly Father and saying, "See? See what I suffered for them? I died for them. Give them My grace." That's one of your intercessors in heaven. One of your principal ones. *The* principal one.

What other intercessor do you have? The Holy Spirit in your soul. The Spirit of Christ is in your soul interceding for you and interceding even for your groanings.[4] Did you know that? I should have brought my Scripture and pointed that out to you. But the Holy Spirit in the soul interprets our groanings. Aren't we Irish people great groaners? Really, aren't we? Do you know we groan our prayers—I do not mean groaning and complaining, but we mumble a great deal. Well, now, the Holy Spirit knows the Irish groanings, and the Holy Spirit is good in Gaelic and interprets all of those groanings and pleadings of our soul. Those are your two great intercessors.

Now the Little Flower says, "I'm going to be one, too, besides our Lord and the Holy Spirit and the Blessed Mother." And she continues:

> This is not impossible that I should spend my
> time in heaven doing good upon earth, since the
> angels in the full enjoyment of the beatific
> vision keep watch over us, I shall never rest till
> the end of the world. But when the angel shall
> have said time is no more, then I shall rest. Then
> I shall rejoice because the number of the elect
> will be complete.

---

4 Cf. Rom 8:26

Do you know that I think perhaps we spend too much time—there must be some—praying for the departed souls and not enough time praying to them? Take for example parents, husbands that are dead, wives, children. They are our intercessors. And perhaps we limit their influence in heaven simply because we do not sufficiently invoke them. So the Little Flower ever wishes very much to be remembered in this way. I can't magine any other saint ever having said, "When I get to heaven, I'm not going to rest, I'm going to work," but she has said it. Therefore, I have great confidence in her. Put her to work! Don't let her rest!

In the Old Testament, in the Book of Jeremiah, God said, "Give Me no rest. Plead with Me night and day!"[5] And that is what our Little Flower is saying. Don't let her sleep! Keep her at work. And may she be mindful of each and every one of your petitions and particularly inspire you not to fear death but to love it. You are going to meet your Lover. You do not realize what a great advantage you have over other people because you have the faith.

Do you want me to tell you something about myself and death? Yes, you do. Alright. I pray every day of my life that I will drop dead in my eightieth year – I'm 78 now – that I will drop dead in my eightieth year in the presence of the Blessed Sacrament on a Saturday (because Saturday is a feast of Our Lady) … or any other feast day of Our Lady. That's what I pray for. I want to see the Good Lord. And maybe I can do a little intercession, too. At any rate,

---

5 This actually comes from Is 43:26.

I'll try. I don't know whether the Good Lord will grant my request to let me drop dead before the Blessed Sacrament on my eightieth birthday, but I can tell you this: That after all the years that I've been asking Him, if He doesn't do it, when He meets me, He's going to be very embarrassed.[B]

༾

Notes

A.   Dross is the waste and impurities that form on the surface of metals such as tin, aluminum, and gold. To remove it, it must be burned off.

B.   Archbishop Sheen got part of his wish. He died Sunday, December 9, 1979, at 7:15 p.m. in his Manhattan home's chapel in front of the Blessed Sacrament. Of course, December 8 is the Feast of the Immaculate Conception. In some ways, it is fitting he did not die on that day but on December 9, the Feast of another great servant of Jesus and Mary, St. Juan Diego. The connection between the Servant of God and St. Juan is especially fitting because, as Pope John Paul II is said to have once noted, the Aztec saint and Mary made the greatest evangelization team in history. The same could also be said of Mary and Archbishop Sheen.

❧ CHAPTER 5 ❧

St. Thérèse and the value of suffering

Now more on our Little Flower and also theology. I hope I can make it clear to you. If not, it will not be because you do not understand it. Remember: Poor teachers are those who do not understand it themselves.

But this is the kind of problem that I am presenting to you about the Little Flower. You would never think, would you, that a very rich man would have need of a few pennies. Our Blessed Lord said those who are well have no need of a physician. Nor would you ever believe that one who was learned and had university degrees would ever have to learn the ABCs.

Could it ever be, then, that our Blessed Lord, who lived on this earth and ascended into heaven is sorrowing? Is our Lord still on the cross? And will He be on the cross until the end of time?

Now I am going to read to you some passages of St.

Thérèse. She has a very unusual point of view. She never looks to our Lord to be consoled. She's always looking to console Him. That's the amazing thing.

I'm going to give you her own words first, and then I'm going to explain this mystery. As a matter of fact, I think she is far closer to the truth than many of our theologians.

Now one passage that I will share with you is this:

> Since our Well-Beloved has trodden the wine press alone, the wine which He gives us to drink in our turn, let us not refuse to wear garments dyed with blood. Let us press out for Jesus a new wine which may slake His thirst [as if our Lord were still thirsty]. And looking around Him, He will no longer be able to say, "He is alone." Neglect, forgetfulness, this I believe is what pains Him the most.

And again in another passage:

> After the exile on earth, I hope to enjoy the possession of You in our eternal Fatherland. But I have no wish to amass merits for heaven. I work for love alone, my sole aim being to console the Sacred Heart. So at the close of life's evening, I shall appear before You with empty hands, and I ask You not to count my works. All I want to do is to console You.

And finally:

See then all that Jesus asks of us? He has no need of our works, but only our love. This very God who declares that He needs not to tell us if He were hungry did not hesitate to beg of the Samaritan woman a little water. He thirsted. But in saying, "Give me to drink," it was the love of this poor creature that the Creator of the universe was seeking. He thirsted for our love, and He wants us to surrender ourselves to Him to make Him happy.

Now you always thought that our Blessed Lord was perfectly happy and needed no consolation. How then does St. Thérèse say that He needs consolation? I shall give you the answer.

When our Blessed Lord was on the cross, He spoke seven times. They were almost like the seven notes of a funeral hymn. And one of the last words He said was, "It is finished."[1]

That did not mean, "Thank heavens, it's over." But it means, "My mission is accomplished. I have done all the Father asked Me to do."

So you see here our Blessed Lord is saying that He has finished the work that He had to do. Now if He had finished His sufferings, how could St. Thérèse say that she has to console Him?

---

1 John 19:30

Well, the answer is this: When our Lord was on the cross, the body He suffered in was the body He took from Mary. The body to which St. Thérèse is referring is His Mystical Body, the Church. In other words, Christ is glorified in heaven in the body He took from Mary, but He is living in His body on earth, and He is suffering many indignities now just as He suffered indignities then.

So our Lord's sufferings were finished in the physical body, but His sufferings are not finished in the Mystical Body, the Church. Now what proves this better than the conversion of St. Paul, whose name before his conversion, as you know, was Saul?

He was a learned man. He had studied under the most learned of the teachers – Gamaliel – and he was the greatest bigot that ever lived.

Armed with letters from Jerusalem, he set out for the city of Damascus to persecute the Church of that city, just as the Church is being persecuted today in eastern Europe.^ Remember this is about five years or more after the ascension of our Lord into heaven, and the whole Church was disturbed about this learned man.

The poor fishermen like Peter and Andrew and James and John could not combat his intelligence. And in all the Christian churches there must have been novenas made saying, "Dear God, dear God, send a good case of coronary thrombosis to Saul! Send someone to answer him." And God said, "All right, I will send someone to answer Saul. I will send Saul!" So during this journey the heavens are opened and the glorified, risen Christ in heaven speaks and says, "Saul! Saul! Why are you persecuting Me?"

"Who are you?"

"I am Jesus, Whom you are persecuting."[2]

Imagine! The glorified Christ in heaven saying, "You're persecuting Me!" How could Saul do that?

Well, if someone steps on your foot, does not your head complain? And what Saul was doing was touching the Body of Christ (which is the Church) and the Head, Christ Himself, complains.

So St. Paul understood this mystery very well. And in his first letter to the Colossians … (Oh, incidentally, I once heard someone reading an epistle to the Philippinos! It was to the Philippians, but this one is to the Colossians.)

Let us listen to St. Paul:

> It is now my happiness to suffer for you. And this is my way of helping you to complete, in my poor human flesh, the full tale of Christ's afflictions still to be endured for the sake of His Body, which is the Church.[3]

In other words, St. Paul is saying that there is a quota of suffering reserved for the Church which is not yet filled

---

2 Acts 9:4-6
3 Col 1:24

up, and I am filling it up in my flesh for the sake of Christ in heaven, for the sake of His Church.

I once had an audience with the Holy Father Paul VI, and I said, "You are well named Paul, because Paul was persecuted very often when he went from city to city, from Lystra to Derby to Antioch of Pisidia ... you are persecuted by your own."

And the Holy Father said, "Yes, I am. I open my mail at midnight, and in every letter is a thorn. When I put my head on my pillow at night, I lay it on a crown of thorns." But then he went on. "But I cannot tell you," he said, "how happy I am to suffer that I might fill up in my flesh"—he was quoting St. Paul—"the sufferings that are still wanting to the Passion of Christ for the sake of His Body, which is the Church."

Now we come back to St. Thérèse. See, St. Thérèse had a deep understanding of Christ. She was not just thinking of Him in heaven. She was thinking of His Passion still enduring in this world. Suffering in His Church? How could that be? How could the cross endure through the centuries?

Mozart was once asked how he ever composed such beautiful music. He said, "Well, I heard all the music at once, and then it took time to unravel it."

Calvary is like that. What we saw on Calvary was the greatest moment of the Passion of Christ in history. To Christ it was all at once, but to us it is worked out successively. Or to give you another example, if you look at a tree that is cut down in the woods, you'll notice a number of rings in the trees. Now those rings go all up and down that tree, but you see only the rings where it has been cut. All that we saw of the Passion of Christ was what appeared on Calvary. But it's running through the centuries.

Think of, for example, the people in sickbeds in one city alone. I once visited a sick woman, and she was bearing her cross beautifully. To me, this was Christ Who was suffering. And I said, "Do you understand that Christ has asked for your human nature? That He is saying to you, 'I cannot suffer again in this human nature which I took from Mary, because it is now glorified. But there are sinners that have to be redeemed. The work of the cross has to go on. So will you give Me your human nature so that I can suffer in you?'" And she said she'd often thought of that.

I was giving a lecture in Florida about two years ago, and I noticed about five or ten people in wheelchairs in front of the stage. I was lecturing in the theatre, and after the lecture, I jumped off the stage to greet the people in the wheelchairs. I saw over against the wall something that looked like a Grecian statue. It was a woman in an iron lung and she was swathed in white. You could not see the arms. She was just wrapped in white. A little motor was supplying air for her iron lung. She said, "I'm a convert of yours."

I said, "I've never seen you before."

"No," she said, "it was from reading your books."

And I said, "How long have you been in the iron lung?"

"Twenty-one years. I was married, and I contracted polio the first year of my marriage. And when my husband discovered it, he left me. But when he left, he pulled out the electric plug that supplies air to my lungs. And a servant saw it and put back the plug. I'm able to move only my head, no other part of my body."

I said, "Do you understand suffering? And how you are continuing the Passion of Christ for the sake of His Body, the Church?"

And she said, "Not too well."

I said, "I shall write to you every day for six months until you get a full understanding of your mission."

Well, at the end of six months, she had completely comprehended it. But she said, "Tell me something more."

I said, "Sometimes lovers squeeze too tight, and the Lord loved you so much, He squeezed you too tight. Did you ever think of what might have happened to you if the Lord had not clipped your wings?" She said, "I should hate to contemplate it."

Now this was the continuation of the Passion of Christ. All of you people who are suffering in any way,

Christ is in you. He's even in those who have not the faith.

As you know, I was in mission work for 16 years, and I was never disturbed at all about the problem of – as they used to put it – how the pagans are saved, even though the gospel had not been preached to them. Believe me, when you walk through the streets of Kolkata[4] and see 250,000 people sleeping in the waste-filled gutters at night, when you see starving mothers with starving children strapped to their backs, you say, "I never saw so many Christs in my life!" Or you might object, "But they do not know Christ!" In a certain sense, they do not need to. Christ is in their suffering. He is not in their vice, not in their knowledge, but He's in their pain.

Don't you think, for example, that Christ was somehow hidden in the six million victims at Auschwitz and Dachau, all those Jews who went to an incinerated death? Though they did not know it and were loyal to the law of Moses even as they understood it, they were in some way continuing unwittingly the Passion of Christ and being saved by it.

I read once a story of someone who had been to Dachau, and he said that one afternoon three gallows were erected in the camp yard. The nooses were put around two men's necks and then around the neck of a boy. The Nazi guards called everyone to attention. The chairs were pulled out from under them, and as the two men died, they shouted, "Long live liberty!"

---

4 Kolkata is the name they now use for Calcutta. The spelling was changed in 2001 to more perfectly reflect the way the locals pronounce the city's name.

But the boy who was hanging, being light, did not die immediately. As he swung loosely, some man behind the author said, "Where is God now?" For a half hour they watched the blue-tinged tongue of the boy and finally he gave a last gasp. Again this voice said, "Where is God now?" And this author said, "There He is! Hanging on the gallows!"

The Passion of Christ is continuing, and the knowledge of this alone makes pain bearable.

During World War I, there was a poet by the name of Stoddard Kennedy, who, as chaplain of the British forces, was very much troubled by the muck and the mud and the trenches and the blood. And he wondered what has all this to do with God? And he writes:

> And I wonder if God sheds tears,
> I wonder if God can be sorrowin' still,
>   And 'as been all these years.
> I wonder if that's what it really means,
>   Not only that 'e once died,
> Not only that 'e came once to earth
>   And wept and were crucified?
> Not just that 'e suffered once for all
>   To save us from our sins,
> And then went up to 'is throne on 'igh
>   To wait till 'is 'eaven begins.
> But what if 'e came to the earth to show,
>   By the paths o' pain that 'e trod,
> The blistering flame of eternal shame
>   That burns in the heart o' God?

See how the whole world changes when you look at it from this point of view, the continuing Passion of Christ? I think everybody in this world is either on the cross or underneath it. On it by discipline, mortification, faith, sharing the Passion of Christ, or underneath it with clenched fists and hatred, begging the Lord to come down from that cross.

Now coming back to the Little Flower, you see the Christ she was consoling was not the Christ that has risen to heaven but the Christ in His totality being denied, for example in Russia and China. This is suffering for Christ: the cancer patients; all those who have had the faith and lost it; the alcoholics; the drug addicts. All of these in some way are tearing at the very Heart of Christ.

A friend of mine spent 14 years in a prison, a communist prison. He continued always to preach Christ in prison, and, therefore, was subjected to all manner of torture. He was put into a cell with starving rats and locked up for five days.

And I said to him, "What did you think about when you were put in a cell with hundreds of starving rats?"

"Well," he said, "As you know, I'm Hebrew, now a Christian. I'm Hebrew and, therefore, I know the Hebrew language. And I went back to the words of our Lord on the cross, "*Eli, Eli, lama sabach-thani.*"

Our Lord spoke those words in Hebrew, "My God,

91

my God, why have You abandoned me?"[5] He said those words are in the past tense, not the present. During His agony on the cross, our Lord was not saying why *are* You abandoning Me, but why *have* You? In the past.

Why did our Lord put this abandonment in the past tense?

First of all because He was absolutely certain of victory. That was the reason. He knew that after the cross would come the empty tomb. And as the Scripture puts it, "having joy set before Him, He endured the cross."[6]

So my friend said, "So I decided to consider the rats as past." And he said, "I've been preaching Christ, I've been suffering for Him: I'm not going to be eaten by these rats! So I will live as if it had happened to me long ago."

And he said when he took that attitude, some of the rats just sat down exhausted from fatigue and philosophized, and others nibbled at the rags on his feet. And at the end of five days, they let him out of the cell filled with starving rats. See, he was able to actualize his sufferings because he related them to the Passion of Christ.

Now to conclude. You see the Little Flower is quite a modern theologian. She gives us the way to understand our Lord. He is in agony still. That is incidentally why we have to revive the devotion to the Sacred Heart. The cross on top of the Sacred Heart and the crown of thorns around

---

5 Ps 22[21]:1; cf. Matt 27:46
6 Heb 12:2

it are what we give to Christ. The flames are what Christ gives to us.

Now with this theology of the Little Flower, your spiritual life will be changed. You will not just be praying for yourselves. You have the world to pray for. You are continuing His redemptive work with the little trials that you have to bear. All of these Christ makes use of and says, "I'm suffering through you, and we are redeeming souls." And as I told you, every soul in the world has a price tag on it.

The Little Flower did not speak so much of the word *reparation*. She spoke of *consolation*. That is what we bring to Christ, consolation, consolation of a good and a virtuous life. There are, you know, only two classes of people in the world as regards love. Some just want love, and they sit and wait for it. It must come to them. They are the unhappy people. The others do not want to be loved, they want to love, to give themselves to others. This is happiness. And now only when we learn to console others, to almost forget ourselves, then only do we become Christ-like.

The one lesson you want to understand is that Christ is using you. He's using you for others. We have to save the Church. We have to save some priests. We have to save some nuns. We have to save the faithful. We have to save the communists. We have to save our country, make it peaceful. All of the sufferings combined can do that.

Whenever there is silence round about me, by day or night, I am startled by a cry. It came down from the cross the first time I heard it. And I went out and searched and found a man in the throes of crucifixion.

And I said, "I will take you down," and I tried to take the nails out of His feet.

But He said, "Let them be. For I cannot be taken down until every man, woman, and child come to take Me down."

But I said, "What can I do? I cannot bear Your cry!"

And He said, "Go into the world and tell everyone that you meet, there is a Man on the cross."

ॐ

Notes

A. Of the estimated 45.5 million Christians martyred in the twentieth century, roughly 70 percent are said to have been killed by communists. It is likely that a large percentage of these were Eastern European Catholics, with many more from among the Russian Orthodox. (Source, Zenit News Service, May 10, 2002; *The Chronicles* magazine, May 19, 2006).

CHAPTER 6

St. Thérèse and the sword

The new way of St. Thérèse is not to start thinking about how wicked you are, how sinful, but to begin looking at our Lord. And from that, you will see that you are not as good as you ought to be, but you will try to please the one you love.

Let me give you some of her words along these lines. She said:

> Jesus! I would so love Him, love Him as He has never been loved in the history of the world.

And one of the novices – for she was the Mistress of Novices – came to her one day, and she said, "Oh, I have so many virtues to acquire."

The Little Flower said, "No, you've got a lot of things to lose!"

That's the trouble. Our spiritual books tell us how to acquire humility. I told you about the 12 ways of St. Bernard. Well now, you'll go crazy trying to develop those 12 ways. One of them is to love to be stomped on and trampled on. The Little Flower says, no, start loving the Lord, and then you'll no longer be proud. You cannot start acquiring, for example, the virtue of humility or fortitude. You can never fall in love with an abstraction. You can only love a person. No one in the world ever fell in love with a theorem of geometry.

This is the trouble with secular humanism and materialism: There's no person to love. So then the new way of the Little Flower is … fall in love. Love the Good Lord, and then you will strive to please Him. And because you see that there are imperfections in you, you will love Him more so that they may be washed away. This is not a little way. It's the new way because we've forgotten it. It's buried in Scripture. It's buried in Isaiah, buried in the Psalms, buried in Zechariah, and she digs it out for us.

Now we come to the second point. What effect did it have on her? Now when we look at the picture of this frail little French girl, we think of her, yes, as the little Thérèse, frail, meek, humble. But does love make one that way? Real lovers are courageous.

Do you know what she wanted to be? She wanted to be a soldier. She used to *dream* about it. In one of her dreams, someone was conscripting soldiers for an army. And she heard a voice saying, "Maybe we ought to ask for Thérèse." And she said, "Well, I'm ready." She said, "I'm sorry it's not a holy war, but I'm ready to fight anyway."

Now we never think of the Little Flower as having a saint whom she wanted to be like more than anyone else, but she did. Do you know who that was? Joan of Arc. Can you imagine her seated on a horse clad in armor? And she said, "If I were Joan of Arc, it would not be voices that I would hear from heaven. It would be only the voice of my Beloved."

One of her favorite texts of Scripture, therefore, was "I came not to bring peace, but the sword."[1] Here, for example, are some excerpts from her writings. First of all about the sword:

> Oh, my Beloved, I understand to what combats You have destined me. It is not on the battlefield I shall fight. I am a prisoner of Your Love. Freely have I riveted the chain which unites me to You and separates me forever from the world. My sword is love and "I shall chase the stranger from the Kingdom. I shall make You to be proclaimed King" in the souls of men.[A]

Those last words of hers were the words of Joshua when he went into the Promised Land.[2] In other words, she was going to have Christ proclaimed as the King.

---

1 Matt 10:34

2 The editors assiduously looked for this quote in the Bible, but found nothing similar, either in reference to Joshua or any other biblical figure. It may be that St. Thérèse was quoting St. Joan of Arc or that she simply composed this line herself in "Prayer Inspired by a Picture of Joan of Arc" (see Endnotes).

And then St. Thérèse said:

> A sister showed me a photograph representing
> Joan of Arc, consoled in a prison by her voices. I,
> too, am consoled by an interior voice. The saints
> encourage me from above, and they say to me,
> "So long as you are in fetters, you cannot fulfill
> your mission. But after your death, then will be
> the time of your conquest."

In other words, she said I'm going to be a warrior
and a soldier after my death. I am in no battlefields now
except the battle of the spiritual life.

This figure gives you some idea of, for example, her
powerful intercession. This, too, accounts for her love of
missions. She is the patroness of the Propagation of the
Faith,[B] though she was never in mission lands. The reason
she is the patroness of the Propagation of the Faith was
because she loved the missions, and she corresponded all
of her life with two missionary priests and offered up her
sufferings for them.[C]

Yes, that is true, but there is a deeper reason still. This
woman was in love, and she wanted her Beloved known
all over the world. That's why she loved the missions! As
she put it:

> Like the prophets and the doctors, I would
> enlighten souls. I would travel the whole world
> to preach Your Name and set up Your glorious
> cross in pagan lands. But one mission could

never suffice for me. Would that I could, at one and the same time, proclaim the gospel to the world, even to the remotest of its islands. I would desire to be a missionary not only for a few years but to have been one from the creation of the world and to continue to the end of time.

Love makes one a missionary. When we cease to love, we cease to be a missionary. Now it is sometimes asked, for example, why is there a decline of conversions today? Is it due to ecumenism? No, *it's not due to ecumenism.* It's due to the fact that we're not making Christ the center of our lives. And if we were deeply in love with Christ instead of with social programs and the like (all which have their place, but here I am speaking of primacy), if we gave the primacy to Christ, then we'd be on fire to save souls. After all, the reason we are tired in body is because we are already tired in mind. We have no love. The fires have gone out. We are cinders, burnt out cinders floating in the immensity of space and time. And here is a young girl. It is almost as if she is locked up in a gilded cage, absolutely straining at the leash in order to become a missionary. Why? Simply because she loved!

As I told you, love does not mean just simply to have and to own and to possess. It's not sitting on the throne waiting for others to serve. It's the going out, the spending of oneself. Love is not the circle circumscribed by self. It's like a cross outstretched to embrace the whole world.

Love isn't Buddha, fat, sleek, a well-oiled body, hands

folded across the breast intently looking inward, thinking only of self. It's the picture of thin saints looking out for the mission to the world, as Thérèse looks out in many of her photos. And therefore, she loved this text, the sword. And she says many times in her writings that "I am entering Carmel to bring the sword to the monastery of Carmel." In other words, it needed a little fire. She entered it to change it. And her reason for doing so was right.

We're very fond of talking peace today, but all we mean by peace is lack of disturbance. Our Lord said, "I came not to bring peace." God HATES PEACE in those who are destined for war! And we are destined for war, spiritual war. We've forgotten that we're in a combat. We are in a *genuine combat*. When our first parents were driven out of the garden of Paradise, God stationed an angel with a flaming sword, a two-edged sword that turned this way and that. Why? To keep our first parents from going back to eat of the Tree of Life and thus immortalize their evil. And the only way we can ever get back again *into* Paradise is by having that sword run into us. It's flaming because it's love. It's two-edged because it cuts, and it penetrates. It's not the sword that's thrust outward to hack off the ear of the servant of the high priest as Peter did. It's the sword that's thrust inward to cut out all of our seven pallbearers of the soul, the pride and covetousness, lust, anger, envy, gluttony, and sloth.

This was the sword she loved. And this sword is what we've forgotten in our modern world with the dropping away of discipline, the ascetic principle. The disciplinary principle of the Christian world has moved to the totalitarian countries. And concerning the sword, I quoted the sword in relationship to the Garden of Eden, but in the prophecy of Zechariah, we read this:

> This is the very word of the Lord of Hosts: Oh sword, awake against my shepherd.[3]

Who is the shepherd? Our Lord. So Zechariah is having the heavenly Father say, "Sword awake! Awake against My shepherd, against My Son, against Him who works with Me." So when our Blessed Lord came to this earth, the sword of Herod was raised against Him. Did anyone ever raise a sword against a two-year-old Caesar? Or a six-month-old Stalin? Why the sword against Him? Because it plays a role in salvation. It belongs to warriors. And as the heavenly Father ran the sword into His own Son, the Son ran the sword into His own Mother. Simeon said to Mary, "You, too, shall be pierced to the heart."[4] So the Father ran a sword into His Son, the Son into His own Mother, and our Lord into us.

"I have come not to bring peace, but the sword." This, then, is the way of the warrior and of the little girl who wanted to be a soldier. And there was not much difference in her mind between a soldier and a missionary.

So summing it all up, you may have your own reasons for calling her way the Little Way. It's alright if it means spiritual childhood, but remember that St. Therese said, "I did not find spiritual childhood in the text of Matthew

---

3 Cf. Zech 13:7
4 Luke 2:35

... 'unless you become as little children.'"⁵ She said that means you're old, and then you become young again.⁶

I think hers is the new way. You'll fall in love. Then you'll discipline yourself. Then you'll be full of zeal. Then when the Lord's work is to be done, you do it. And when we're not in love, we're tired, and we're exhausted. Because she was full of love, the particular action that appealed to her was that of the soldier and the missionary. This is the new vision of sanctity. It needs to be revived in our day.

When Joshua had just crossed over the Jordan and was about to enter into the Promised Land, he saw before him a man with a sword. And Joshua, the leader of the Jews was frightened. He said, "Are you with me or are you against me?"

Those seemed to be the only two alternatives. Entering into the land of the Canaanites, who was this man? For or against?

And the answer came back, "Nay! I am the Commander of the Lord of Hosts!"⁷

It was the prefigurement of Christ with the sword. Those who have been loyal to the Commander of the Lord

---

5 Cf. Matt 18:3

6 To appreciate this, refer back to Chapter 2, where the archbishop explains that as a person gets older in chronological age, they become "younger" because they get back closer to the source of life, Who is God.

7 Cf. Josh 5:13-14. The commander – also translated as "the prince of the hosts of the Lord" – has been thought by some to be St. Michael the Archangel, who Rev 12:7 tells us leads the Lord's armies.

of Hosts with the sword are those who bear it in the battle against evil in the evangelization of the world, and who bear it simply because they followed the new way, which is the old way, really, the biblical way, of falling in love with Christ, first and foremost.

Augustine was right: Give me a man who has loved, and I will tell him what God is.[8] So begin to love. Not only your happiness will increase, but also your zeal. This, my friends, is the new way, which is the old way.

Notes

A. This is from a prayer inspired by St. Thérèse's seeing a statue of St. Joan of Arc:

O Lord God of Hosts, who hast said in Thy Gospel: "I am not come to bring peace but a sword" (Matt 10:34), arm me for the combat. I burn to do battle for Thy Glory, but I pray Thee to enliven my courage. . . . Then with holy David I shall be able to exclaim: "Thou alone art my shield; it is Thou, O Lord, Who teachest my hands to fight" (Ps 144[143]:1–2).

O my Beloved, I know the warfare in which I am to engage; it is not on the open field I shall fight. . . I am a prisoner held captive by Thy Love; of my own free will I have riveted the fetters which bind me to Thee, and cut

8 Cf. *De Trinitate* (On the Trinity) Book 8, Chapter 8, paragraph 12, St. Augustine (cite: http://www.newadvent.org/fathers/130108.htm).

me off for ever from the world. My sword is Love! with it—like Joan of Arc—"I will drive the strangers from the land, and I will have Thee proclaimed King"—over the Kingdom of souls.

Of a truth Thou hast no need of so weak an instrument as I, but Joan, Thy chaste and valiant spouse, has said: "We must do battle before God gives the victory." O my Jesus! I will do battle, then, for Thy love, until the evening of my life. As Thou didst not will to enjoy rest upon earth, I wish to follow Thy example; and then this promise which came from Thy sacred lips will be fulfilled in me: "If any man minister to Me, let him follow Me, and where I am there also shall My servant be, and . . . him will My Father honor" (John 12:26). To be with Thee, to be in Thee, that is my one desire; this promise of fulfillment, which Thou dost give, helps me to bear with my exile as I wait the joyous Eternal Day when I shall see Thee face to face. Amen.

B.   This is both the previously mentioned missionary society and a dicastery in the curia of the Holy See, formerly known as the Congregation for the Propagation of the Faith and today officially known as Congregation for the Evangelization of Peoples.

C.   The first was Maurice Bartolomeo Belliere, who at the time was a seminarian for the diocese of Bayeux, France. On September 29, 1897, the eve of Thérèse's death, he embarked for Algeria, where he entered the novitiate of the White Fathers. After some years as a missionary in Africa, he contracted a disease and returned to France. He died July 14, 1907, at the age of 33 years old.

The other was Adolphe Roulland, a seminarian of the Society of the Foreign Missions of Paris. Ordained to the priesthood on June 28, 1896, he departed for China on August 2 of the same year. In 1909, he returned to France, where he had various assignments. He died June 12, 1934.

❧ CHAPTER 7 ❧

St. Thérèse, God, and our relationship with Him

My dear friends, in this meditation I am going to try to describe to you what it means to be a Christian and what it means to be a saint.

First of all, how did Christ come to be on this earth? Well, one day an angel came out from the great white throne of light and came down to a virgin kneeling in prayer and said to her, "Will you give God a human nature?" When she discovered that she was not to lose her virginity to give God a human nature, she agreed.[1] So God then took from this woman a human nature through which He taught us, He governed us, and He sanctified us.

One day, maybe while we were yet infants, we were called by God and asked, "Will you give Me your human nature?" God wishes to continue the Incarnation. As Mary

---

1 Cf. Luke 1:28-38

gave Him a human nature, He continues His Incarnation by us giving Him a human nature. Now this had to happen, too, to the Little Flower. From her earliest memories, she always wanted to be God's. So she always offered to Him her human nature. Now, not every one of us gives our human nature to God in the same way. She gave hers completely and totally.

Let me give you an example of a pencil. A pencil is very supple and flexible in my hand. If I want the pencil to write the word "God," it will write the word "God." It's totally subservient and obedient to my will.

Suppose, however, this pencil had a will of its own. When I wanted to write the word "God," it might write the word "dog." I couldn't do anything with it. And why? Because this pencil would not be completely obedient to my person. And so, not every one of us gives our human nature to God in such a way that He can use it totally and completely. We hold back!

One of the disturbing things in our modern world is, for example, that young people should be concerned with what they call the problem of identity. "Who am I?" Can you imagine living 15, 20, 25 years not knowing who we are?[A]

When are we happy, really? We are happy when we give our human nature to someone else. In marriage, for example, man gives himself to a woman. In religion, we give ourselves to Christ. In the Little Flower, there was never any question of Thérèse wanting to be Thérèse. She never had a problem of identity. She just wanted to be His, and to be His so totally and completely that anything the Good Lord wanted to do with her, He could do.

A Russian novelist once wrote of himself. He said when he was in Siberia, "If God wants to use me to stuff up an old rat hole, I'm very willing." Now God doesn't use us all in exactly the same way, just as the director of an orchestra does not use every musician in the same way. And in a drama, the actors play different roles.

But when the curtain goes down, we're not asked what role we played, we are asked how well we played the role assigned to us. So if we give ourselves completely to God, to Christ, then we've played the role well.

Now coming back to the Little Flower, she gave herself so perfectly to the Good Lord. Did you know she sent out a kind of a wedding invitation? She wrote it out one day because she was going to give herself to her Divine Spouse. This was prompted by a cousin of hers who was being married. The invitation she sent out said you will not able to attend the ceremony, but there will come an eventual day when we get back from our honeymoon – that is, at the end of time – when you will meet us.

Now this is the invitation that she sent out. She wrote it apropos of the marriage of her cousin. And she writes in her own story eight days afterwards, "My cousin Jean got married, and I can't tell you how anxious I was to learn her example about all the attentions which as a bride she lavished on her bridegroom. And I wanted to know all

I could about it because surely my attitude toward our Lord ought not to be less carefully studied than Jean's attitude toward her husband. So I amused myself by sketching out a wedding invitation of my own modeled on hers."

So she's the bride. Who's the Bridegroom? It's Christ. She's not going to belong to anyone else. And this was the little sketch that she wrote:

> Almighty God, Creator of heaven and earth,
> Lord of the whole world and the glorious Virgin
> Mary, Queen of the Heavenly Court, invite you
> to take part in the wedding of their Son, Jesus
> Christ, King of Kings, Lord of Lords, to Thérèse
> Martin. Now invested by the right of dowry
> with two freedoms, Monsieur Louis Martin, the
> heir and chief of the misfortune and the
> humiliation, and Madame Martin, lady in
> waiting, invite you to take part in the wedding
> of their daughter Thérèse to the Lord Jesus.

We don't think generally, you know, of souls being so completely dedicated to the Good Lord that to them it is a wedding. Thérèse must have been, therefore, a rather playful little spirit to ever have thought of a wedding in these particular terms. And then she goes on to say:

> You are not able to be present at the
> announcement [that is to say the day of her
> Final Vows], but [she said] the Lord is coming
> on the last day. And when He comes, then we
> will celebrate the wedding together.

Now this does not mean that anyone in this life, for example, who is committed to a human vow is any less Christ's. Remember that married love does not stand in the way of Christ's love. The only difference between, for example, priests and religious who have committed themselves completely to God and the married people is that we give ourselves directly to Him, and the married give themselves indirectly. But they are His. Totally.

Now suppose that a number of worldly people read this sermon up to this point. Suppose they saw a picture of this young girl who dies at 24 years of age and are struck by – well, certainly – the purity of her expression and a beauty to which one cannot be totally indifferent. What would the worldly person say about anyone giving oneself so completely to Christ that she writes out a wedding invitation?

They would say, "It's a waste! Think of the good she could have done in the world! Wouldn't she have been a wonderful wife?! Maybe she could have done social work!"

That would have been their argument. But remember that, in the divine order, some lives *have* to be wasted, wasted from the worldly point of view.

Take, for example, Mary of Bethany. Our Lord was seated at table in the house of Simon the leper and Pharisee for a banquet to celebrate Jesus' raising her brother Lazarus from the dead. Her sister Martha served the meal. Mary now enters with a jar of costly perfume made from genuine aromatic nard.

She stands over the feet of our Lord. She breaks the vessel of precious ointment. It was a custom very often among the Jews to break a vessel of precious ointment over a dead body and then to throw the remains of the glass into the coffin. Well, she breaks this vessel of precious ointment over the feet of our Blessed Lord. Judas, who was there, says, "Why all this waste? It could have been sold for 300 *denarii* and given to the poor."[2]

Our Lord immediately came to the defense of that waste, saying, "Leave her alone." And because our Lord was within 10 days of the crucifixion, he added, "She's done it for My burial."[3]

In other words, there are certain things in life that we waste; we are seemingly prodigal about them. The Little Flower was that way about her own life, just as this pious woman, Mary, was prodigal about the giving of precious perfume.

Take, for another example, King David who lived a thousand years before Christ and who was the model of the Kingship of Christ.

King David was fighting a battle against the Philistines near his old home town, which was Bethlehem, where

---

2 Cf. Matt 26:6-13; Mark 14:3-9; Luke 7:36-38; John 12:1-8; a *denarius* (*denarii* is the plural of *denarius*) was a piece of silver, and was an average man's daily wage.
3 Cf. Mark 14:8

Christ was to be born a thousand years later. Many a man, when he goes back to his boyhood town, has memories of what happened there. He had recollections of the water of Bethlehem, and he said, "If I could only have some of that water from the well of Bethlehem." But the enemy line was between himself and that well whose waters he tasted when he was a boy.

A few of his brave soldiers said, "We'll go through the lines and get the water!" And they did. They went through the enemy lines and brought back the water. When they did, David took the vessel of water and poured it out. He said, "Water purchased at such a sacrifice cannot be taken as a drink."[4] If he had drunk that water, we would not be telling that story now. But to him it became precious because it was offered in sacrifice.

You see, gold that is hoarded makes one a miser. Knowledge that is selfishly possessed makes one proud. Flesh that is too cared for turns into lust. It is the things that are spent, wasted for God's sake that become remembered through history.

We tell the story of David because he "wasted" the water as the woman "wasted" the perfume and as the Little Flower was "wasting" her life on Christ. This is the secret of being a good Christian, to be His. What difference does it make, really, what we're doing? Too often we think that we have to be in a noble position to please the Good Lord.

---

4 Cf. 2 Sam 23:13-17 (Note: In the Douay-Rheims Bible, 2 Sam is 1 Kings.)

Remember when the Lord gave ten talents, five talents, one talent as gifts?[5] Who buried the talent? The one with the ten? The one with the five? No, it was he who received one talent. He said, "Well, I don't have very much. I'm not worth anything, so I'll bury it."

But our Lord held him responsible for that one talent. We may not have a very important position in the world, but at least we have one talent. And if we use it in a Christ-like way, it will be wasted, wasted for Christ. This is really how we get strength.

Now, I do a great deal of talking. In priest retreats, I talk five times a day for four or five days straight and 35-40 minutes each time. Well, that takes a lot of energy out of a 39 year old man. Why do you laugh?

And so some people would say, "Well, why do you do this? Why do you spend yourself?" It's simply because the Lord wants me to do it. I can't ignite any fires if I sit. That was one of the reasons why, when I first started teaching at Westminster Seminary, London, England in 1924,[B] I took a resolution that in teaching I would never sit, I would always stand. If the students had to stand for me, I would stand for them.

The point is that as we spend our energy, we get it back. The Little Flower took goodness, virginity, sweetness, innocence, and wasted it all unseen, but now it comes back a hundred-thousand fold. If the wheat is kept in the barn,

---

5 Cf. Matt 25:14-30

it's wasted.[C] It's when we save ourselves that we begin to lose power. This, then, is how the Incarnation is continued, and may you all be flexible, supple, obedient instruments of the Good Lord. Very often during the day, pray to Him to use you.

Now I often do that. If I go out for a walk, I will often say to the Good Lord, "All right, now use me." Well, He does use me, and it costs me a lot of money generally, but He uses me. I'll run into people who need it badly or someone who is sick. But we have to offer ourselves as pencils. Let Him write poetry. Let Him write prose. Let Him scribble. What difference does it make? This is happiness.

Remember how St. Paul put it in the conclusion to his Letter to the Romans at the end of the eighth chapter. This is one of the really magnificent passages of the New Testament.

St. Paul says Christ has died for us. "Then what can separate us from the love of Christ? Can affliction or hardship? Can persecution, hunger, nakedness, peril of the sword? 'We are being done to death for Thy sake all day long,' as Scripture says ... For I am convinced that there is nothing in death or life, in the realm of spirits or super-human powers, in the world as it is or the world as it shall be, in the forces of the universe, in heights or depths, nothing in all creation that can separate us from the love of God in Christ Jesus our Lord."[6]

---

6 Rom 8:35-38

So my good people, waste your life occasionally. Give and it will be given to you. Spend and you'll get something back. In fact, in the divine order the only way to get power is to lose it. Really. If we hoard our strength, we lose it. Give it in the service of neighbor, and we will get it back. The Good Lord will never be outdone in generosity. Carry away with you then the example of the pencil, and let the Lord write with you. He will communicate messages through you. You will do good to others in His Name, visit the sick, help the poor, console the afflicted. This is prolonging the Incarnation.

You read this book to receive strength, but then when you have received it, you have to spend it. As you waste your life, then you'll become richer and richer in the Kingdom of God.

cჯ๏

Notes

A.   In the era in which these talks were made, many young people made trips, the twentieth century version of the Grand Tour, in order to "find themselves." This simply meant they were trying to discover where they wanted to be in life, and who they wanted to be when they got there. This can be a legitimate aim.

However, the notion took on the air of the ridiculous because its eventual prevalence among the young indicated not so much a desire to know oneself but rather a desire

116

to not grow up.

Sheen seems to indicate that the answer to the question of "Who am I?" is already known even before the question is spoken. These people already know who they are. What they really want to know is the more fundamental inquiry, which is left unasked: How will I be happy in this life?

B.   This might confuse some who are familiar with the archbishop's story. Many know he taught at St. Edmund College near Ware, England. How, then, could he have taught at both St. Edmund and Westminster Seminary? From 1904 through 1975, Allen Hall, the Diocese of Westminster's seminary, was located at St. Edmund, and, since he taught Theology, the classes Sheen taught were at the seminary.

C.   Here the archbishop is using the wheat as a figure of speech to represent our span of life on earth. If a person tries to keep it for themselves, to use in their own selfish manner, it's like storing the wheat in the barn. But there it will only decay and in the end produce nothing.

However, if we lavishly give the wheat away, it can be made into bread, which will keep people from starving, it can be given away to the poor so that they may plant their own fields, etc.

By analogy, what the bishop wants us to realize is that anyone who tries to keep their life for themselves and use it very selfishly (i.e., in a manner that keeps it "protected" and "saved up") they will eventually end up with nothing in terms of an eternal reward.

However, if one spends one's life in what the *world* would call a "wasteful way," that is, by using it to serve God and others, in the eyes of God, that would be the life that is worth living.

Thus, the archbishop's statement is made with a sense of irony and almost sarcasm. It is like when he used to encourage priests to make a eucharistic Holy Hour every day. Those who objected to his suggestion would say, "I can't go waste an hour in chapel." To this he would sarcastically reply, "Go and 'waste' an hour before the Blessed Sacrament."

The contrast is seen in the fact that what the world considered a waste (namely that the Little Flower did not spend her life in a worldly way such as in romance or career but kept her life for God in hidden seclusion), God saw as a great offering. It was in no way wasted in His eyes.

Sheen's axiom is simply another way of saying what Our Lord taught: "Anyone who tries to save his life in this world will lose it. But anyone who loses his life for My sake and for the Gospel's sake will find it" (Mark 8:35).

✂ CHAPTER 8 ✄

St. Thérèse and fighting Satan

My dear friends in Christ, there are 10,000 times 10,000 roads down which you may travel during life. But at the end of all of those roads, you will see one or the other of two faces: the merciful face of Christ or the miserable face of Satan. We are living in days of combat, and as we celebrate the life of the Little Flower, we are apt to think that even a saintly life isn't immune from conflict with evil. No one is.

So let me tell you something about her life in relationship to the diabolic. Then I will go on to explain it to you and the nature of our times.

The Little Flower first of all suffered many temptations from the devil at the moment of her death. She said the devil was slithering around, and she suffered so much that she could only commend herself to the Blessed Mother to pronounce the Holy Name of Jesus. She told of a dream she had which manifested, incidentally, her tremendous power over Satan. We need not be fearful of him if we belong to the Lord, as this dream proves.

In this dream, she saw in the garden of the monastery a big barrel, and two little devils appeared over the top of the barrel. She moved toward the barrel, and the devils went down into the barrel. She got closer and looked down, and they jumped out of the barrel and went into the laundry room. They were at one of the windows, and she went to the window to look at them, and the closer she got to them, the farther they got away. They were fearful of her because she was holy.

There are, in fact, several other instances of her conflict with the devil. I will just mention two, one taken from her life and the other taken from a letter she wrote to a friend of hers.

During temptations against faith, she wrote:

> On each fresh occasion of combat when the devil desires to challenge me, I conduct myself valiantly, knowing that to fight a duel is an unworthy act. I turn my back upon the adversary without ever looking him in the face. Then I am ready to run to Jesus and tell Him I am ready to shed every drop of blood in testimony of my belief that there is a heaven.

Then later on in a letter to her cousin:

> The demon, traitor that he is, knows well that

he cannot make a soul who wills to belong
wholly to the good God to commit sin.
Therefore, he endeavors to persuade her that she
sins. That is a great deal gained. But it is not yet
enough to satisfy his rage. He aims at something
further. He wants to deprive Jesus of a beloved
tabernacle. Not being able himself to enter into
the sanctuary, he wishes that it may at least
remain empty and without its Lord. What will
become of such a heart? When the devil has
succeeded in driving away a soul from Holy
Communion, he has gained his ends, and Jesus
weeps.

And on another occasion she said:

I can very well understand why so many people
in the world commit suicide. It is because they
are without faith, and the devil has driven them
to despair.

We're talking about the devil to remind you that we
must be very conscious of this as Thérèse was conscious of
it in her own life. Our theologians are not writing about
the devil. They are quiet about Satan today. Why? Because
Satan is strong when he is not recognized. God's definition
of Himself is: I AM WHO AM. The devil's definition of
himself is: I AM WHO AM NOT. If you want to know
about the devil today, you have to go to poets or literary
experts, not to theologians. Remember when the great
William Butler Yeats spoke of some great monster being
ready to be born at Bethlehem? They are fearful of a very

personal influence in the world, and I do hope that our theologians catch up to the reality of this struggle.

Now in order that we may be on very safe ground in discussing this important subject, I am going to treat it first of all from the psychiatric point of view and secondly from the biblical point of view.

First, let's explore the psychiatric or the psychological point of view. Though our theologians are not writing about the devil, the psychiatrists are. Dr. Rollo May of the Rockefeller Institute has three chapters on the devil in his treatise on psychiatry. Think of it! How does *he* define the diabolic? He analyzes the word "diabolic" into the Greek words *dia ballein*, a tearing apart, a rending asunder.[A] Anything, he said, which splits unity, which fragments, which destroys community, which breaks up pattern, that is the diabolic.

We are all very conscious of how much there has been a disruption of unity in the Church, in religious communities, among ourselves, among the learned, and the unlearned. This, according to the psychiatrist, is the mark of diabolic influence. Three manifestations, he said, are always evidenced in the diabolic.

First is nudity. Nudity, he says, takes the place of love. There is a search only for the experience, not for the love of a person. Every diabolic age, therefore, he says, is the age of the erotic.

Secondly, wherever there is a diabolic age there is

also violence and aggressiveness. You need only recall our modern situation to find proof of this statement.

Thirdly, the diabolic appears with split mind, what May calls schizophrenic mentalities, minds that are divided, uncertain, dubious.

These are the three marks: immorality, violence, and distraught minds. This psychiatrist does not refer to the Bible in order to find an illustration of this. But you remember that when our Blessed Lord went into the land of the Gadarenes, there was a young man possessed of the devil. First thing the Gospel notes about him, he was naked. Secondly, he was violent. Though they bound him with chains, he broke the chains. Thirdly, his mind was split. For example, our Blessed Lord said to him, "What is your name?"

He responded, "My name is Legion."[1]

Now a Legion was 6,000 soldiers in the Roman army. "My name is Legion, for we are many." See, there was no unified personality. "MY name ... for WE are many." In other words, this young man in the land of the Gadarenes had exactly the characteristics of the demonic as depicted by this celebrated psychiatrist.

Now let us turn from the psychiatric to the biblical. What is the satanic in Scripture, particularly in the New Testament? I will not tell you what it is until I come to the

---

1 Cf. Matt 8:28-34; Mark 5:1-6

conclusion of this picture and illustration.

Our Blessed Lord was in the pagan city of Caesarea Philippi, where He asked the most important question that can ever be asked. "Who do you say that I am?"

It was Peter who gave the right answer. He said, "Thou are the Christ, the Son of the living God."

Our Blessed Lord reminded him that he did not know this through his own power. The heavenly Father revealed it to him. Then our Lord gave to Peter the keys.[2] Then comes the text that we hardly ever refer to. We did not even have it in *our* seminaries. We took up this text of the sixteenth chapter of Matthew and completely abandoned what follows. What is it that follows?

Our Lord said, "Now I must go up to Jerusalem to be delivered over to the Gentiles, be spat upon, crucified, and on the third day be raised again from the dead."[3]

In other words, He said He had to suffer.

Now just as soon as our Lord said that, Peter, the head of the Church, took our Lord by the robe and said, "This shall not be!"[4]

We are willing to have a divine Christ but we are not willing to have a suffering one. And our Blessed Lord

---

2 Cf. Matt 16:15-20
3 Cf. Matt 16:21
4 Cf. Matt 16:22

turned on him and said, "Get behind Me, Satan! Do not try to lead Me. I lead YOU, Satan!"[5]

Imagine, Peter is Satan! Personally Satan. It's a frightening thought. Why did our Lord call him Satan? Well, go back to the beginning of our Lord's public life. When He was on the mount of temptation, the devil came to him with three different temptations (or shortcuts) from the cross.[6] Now you know the temptations very well, but I'm going to translate them into modern idiom to bring them up to date.

The first temptation of Satan against our Blessed Lord was this: "You have not eaten in 40 days. You are hungry. See those little rocks down there? They look like loaves of bread. Turn them into bread! People don't want a cross. They've got instincts—sex instinct, hunger instinct, power instinct. They only want their gullets satisfied. Give them bread! Let them have their options. You need no cross." That was the first temptation.

The second temptation. Men love marvels, wonders. Something that will make them say, "Oh, fly to the moon." "Throw Yourself from high atop a steeple unhurt. In three weeks they'll not remember Your name, but give them another marvel. This is what people want! Excitement, something that satisfies their desire for the novelty, the new. But they do not want a cross. Give them wonders, and they'll believe You."

---

5 Cf. Matt 16:23
6 Cf. Matt 4:1-11

And the third temptation of Satan from the cross was: theology is politics. People are not interested in God. The only reality there *is* the political order. And Satan, as it were, holding the tiny globe of the earth in his hand, said to our Lord, "All these kingdoms are *mine*. They are mine!" (Was he telling the truth for once?) And I will give them to You if, falling down, You will adore me. No adoration for the God above ME!" Politics! Three temptations from the cross. That is the business of Satan.

Now let us go back to Peter. Why did our Lord call St. Peter "Satan?" Because St. Peter was doing exactly the same thing that Satan did by tempting Him away from the cross. Our Lord said He had to go to the cross. Peter said, *"No."* Our Lord said, "Therefore, you're Satan."

This is the essence of the satanic, the hatred of the cross. How manifest it is in the world today where there is little restraint, self-discipline, mortification. The ascetic principle of Christianity, the principle of self-denial, has passed to Russia and China, passed out of Christianity to Russia and China (i.e., communism). That's where there is discipline, order, commitment to a common purpose. But it's a destructive discipline because it regards persons as so many grapes to be squeezed to make the collective wine of the State. But at any rate, they have picked up what we have dropped. The cross. It's frightening how the cross is being dropped.

It has not been dropped everywhere. In evidence of it, I received a telephone call one day from a Jewish jeweler whom I had known for 25 years. He said, "I have a hundred silver crucifixes. Would you like to have them?"

I went down to see him, and he had them all in a bag. I said, "Where did you get these?"

He said, "From the nuns. They're not going to wear them anymore. They say the crucifixes separate them from the people. And they wanted to know how much I would give them for the silver." And as this Jewish man put it, "I weighed them out 30 pieces of silver."

And then he turned to me and said, "What's wrong with your Church? I thought the cross meant something to you!"

So I told him what was wrong with the Church, what I'm telling you. Three months later I received him into the Church.

But now you know the nature of the satanic or the diabolic. From a natural point of view it manifests itself in the three ways I mentioned, and from the biblical point of view, it is the hatred of the cross of Christ.

Let me tell you now how differently our Lord and Satan operate as regards the temptation, before and after. Before a temptation or a trial, our Lord appears as an adversary. There's His cross, and as Francis Thompson put it, "He asks, 'Must all thy harvest fields be dunged with rotten death?'"[B] In other words, do you have to fertilize a field with death before there can be life?

And so Christ seems to bar the way. Here we want the release of flesh, more alcohol, drugs, or a broken marriage, whatever it is. And our Lord stands there in the way. And where is Satan? Ah, he's our defender. Our *defender.* He says, "Haven't you heard about the Vatican Council? All this has been changed. Why, you're behind the times! You mean you're still a virgin? You haven't tasted LSD? Haven't you begun to live?"

But then after the fall, our Lord is our Friend, and Satan is our adversary. Our Lord is our Friend. If your sins are as scarlet, they shall be made white as snow.[7] If they are as red as crimson, they shall be made white as wool.[8] If you have sinned seventy times seven, your sins can still be forgiven.[9] We need only take one drop of blood from Him and His cross for salvation.

Our Lord is then our Friend, but Satan now, after the fall, well, why bother now? You've taken your drugs. You've taken up alcohol. You've gone in for adultery. You might just as well continue. No hope now, as one of the characters in the novel *Crime and Punishment* by Dostoevsky the great Russian said. Raskolnikov was his name. *Raskol* in Hebrew means protest.

Now Raskolnikov murdered an old woman for no reason at all. He took no money. He just wanted to snap his fingers at virtue and do the vicious thing for the sake of being vicious. He was in love with a girl by the name of Sonia, a prostitute. And he said to Sonia, who was as

---

7 Cf. Ps 51(50):9
8 Cf. Is 1:18
9 Cf. Matt 18:22

wicked as he was, "Do you know what's going to happen to you, Sonia? One of three things. You're going to throw yourself off a bridge, or you're going to cut your throat, or you will go mad."

What did Sonia do? She picked up her Bible, and she read chapter 11 of John about the resurrection of Lazarus. And she said, "No, I need not do any of these things. After all my sins, I can be reborn in Christ." And she was. Then she brought Raskolnikov back to the Good Lord. And when he was in exile in Siberia, he said that from Sonia and her Christ he even learned to be kind to enemies.

So after we fall, Christ is our Friend, but Satan would drive us, if possible, into despair. And what I fear most about drugs and anything else that destroys consciousness is that it makes possible an inroad for the demonic.

One of our most celebrated experts in drugs is a Jewish scientist named Dr. Cohen.[c] Dr. Cohen has written several books on drug addiction, and this is one of his reflections.

He said that in insanity, where there are no drugs, the hallucinations always come from the experiences of the person himself. That is to say, out of his own background. But, he said, when you are dealing with a drug addict, their hallucinations come from an alien mind, in other words, the demonic.

Now my good people, you live in a land of faith here. You are in one of the safest spots on God's earth at the present time. But I am giving you a more general picture. We are going to get into the age of the demonic, and it will be a great trial for us. And St. Paul, in his letter to the Thessalonians, speaks of this. For example:

> You must now be aware of the restraining hand which insures that he shall be revealed only at the proper time.[10]

What that restraining hand is, we do not know. Is it God's Hand or what? Is it an angel's?

He continues:

> For already the secret power of wickedness is at work. Secret only for the present until the Restrainer disappears from the scene. And then the wicked man [sic] will be revealed, that wicked man whom the Lord Jesus will destroy with the breath of His mouth and annihilate by the radiance of His coming.[11]

We are not in the age of the end of the world. That is not what I am saying. I am only saying that we are in an age where the devil is given a very long rope. And as the Book of Revelation says, the devil knows his time is short, so he has to work fast.

One of my converts, Mrs. Luce,[D] went out to Hollywood to do a play, and I was talking to her on the

---

10 2 Thes 2:6
11 2 Thes 2:7-8

phone, and I said to her, "Clare, have you met the devil in Hollywood?"

And she said, "No, the devil sleeps here."

In other words, he hasn't any work to do there. Everything is easy for him. He just sleeps in Hollywood.

But in conclusion, if our good St. Thérèse faced this combat of evil even at her deathbed, you may be sure that the devil is real. And even though some in the Church may not be as conscious of this influence as those outside, let me assure you, it is real. That is why our emphasis *has* to be on the Person of Christ.

Let me tell you what the most powerful influences are against the demonic.

First of all, the Holy Name of Jesus. At that Name every knee bows, above the earth and under the earth. Secondly, His Precious Blood. We do not have an adequate devotion to the Blood of Christ. But these are the two great arms, the Holy Name of Jesus and invoking the Blood of Christ.

And remember this, too, that evil is relational. That is to say you can only understand evil in relationship to the good. An alcoholic for example does not understand sobriety. A person can be so sick with a fever he may think he's well. You'll never understand what evil is until you know something about goodness. Who for example is most offended by a sour note during a solo? Someone who knows something about music. Who, for example, would be a bit scandalized at a speaker who used bad grammar? Only those who knew grammar. And so evil is understood always in relationship to the good.

Now you don't have to worry about your combat with the devil as immediate. You are under the influence of Christ and His Mother and the intercession of St. Thérèse, so I have not taken a frightening point of view. I tried to give you the satanic and diabolical as something theologically and biblically sound, that you may appreciate we are in this world to do battle. I would like to see restored the prayer that we used to say:[E]

> "St. Michael the Archangel, defend us in battle.
> Be our protection against the malice and snares
> of the devil. May God rebuke him, we humbly
> pray. And do thou, O Prince of the Heavenly
> Host, by the Divine Power, cast into hell Satan
> and the other evil spirits who roam through the
> world seeking the ruin of souls."

And to conclude, as I said in the beginning, you may take 10,000 times 10,000 different roads, and at the end of all of those roads you are going to meet either the merciful Face of Christ or that tragic face of Satan. And one of them is going to say about us … "Mine! Mine!" I know your answer. I know mine. You are His. You will always be His. Fear not the battle. Why, you have already won! Only the news has not yet leaked out.

❧

Notes

A.   The literal Greek root of diabolic (from the Greek words *dia ballein*) mean "thrown through" or "thrown apart." In other words, the devil always tries to destroy the unity that God's love creates. Archbishop Sheen is here amplifying the meaning by speaking of "tearing apart" or "rending asunder" the unity of love.

B.   *Hound of Heaven*, by Francis Thompson (1859-1907).

C.   Sheen here refers to Dr. Sidney Cohen, who taught at University of California, Los Angeles, and was one of the first to study LSD and its effects. He died in 1987 at the age of 76.

D.   Clare Booth Luce, wife of *Time, Sports Illustrated, Fortune,* and *Life* publisher Henry Luce, and herself editor of *Vanity Fair.*

Booth Luce was one of the most remarkable women in America's history (and yet today she is virtually forgotten, at least relative to who she was while living). She was a successful and talented playwright, a screenwriter, a war correspondent (whose articles for *Life* magazine actually effected the execution of World War II in the Far East), a congresswoman, an ambassador to Italy (where she helped check communist power and resolve a border dispute between Italy and Yugoslavia), and three-time author. One of these was a book still in print called *Saints for Now,* where some of the day's prominent authors and figures wrote about saints who had influenced their lives. She both edited and contributed to the work.

Sheen, of course, knew her as "one of my converts." Her only child, a daughter named Ann from her first marriage, died in 1944 from injuries sustained in a car accident while she was a senior at Stanford. This drove Booth Luce to study life's deepest questions, and in the process, her friend Sheen led her into the Catholic Church.

She died in 1987. Her legacy lives on in the Clara Booth Luce Policy Institute (www.cblpi.org).

E.   Here Sheen means "used to say at the end of the Low Mass." For those unfamiliar with the Mass before the Second Vatican Council, there were two basic Masses, the Low Mass and the High Mass. The difference between the two was, essentially, that the High Mass had music (chant, polyphony, hymns, etc.) during the liturgy (e.g., a sung Gloria and Agnus Dei) and incense, whereas the Low Mass did not.

At the end of the Low Mass, there were said the prayers implemented for the whole Church by Pope Leo XIII (1878-1903) following the example of Bl. Pius IX: Three Hail Marys; one Hail, Holy Queen; one Prayer to St. Michael the Archangel (which Leo wrote after a vision showing God allowing Satan free reign throughout the twentieth century); and a Collect.

In 1934, Pius XI ordained that the intention for these prayers was the conversion of Russia. With the removal of the distinctions between High and Low Mass after Vatican II, these so-called Leonine prayers went by the wayside for some reason, although pastors still have the option of having them recited. Of course, there is nothing to stop individual lay members of God's Church from saying these on their own after Mass or at any time.

St. Thérèse and suffering for the sake of Love

Those of you who have been following these thoughts on the Little Flower will recall how closely we have tied her life up either with Scripture or with the life of our Blessed Lord. We will do the same in this chapter, and our point will be to show how the Little Flower imitated the Good Lord in what we will call *transference*. Now do not let me confuse you at the very beginning by that word. I shall explain it right away.

Just suppose that you were in debt, and there was no possible way of getting out of debt. Some friend comes to you and says, "I will pay your debt." That would be a financial transference. He would be taking your burden upon himself.

To give you another example, perhaps you have seen the picture of a little boy carrying another boy on his back, and the boy on the back is a cripple. And the boy who was carrying him said, "No, he's not heavy, he's my brother." That's transference, too.

Now let us apply transference to our Blessed Lord, and then we will apply it to the Little Flower.

First of all, to our Blessed Lord. He transferred to Himself three kinds of evils that we have in this world: physical, which includes all manner of sickness and disease; secondly, mental sufferings; and thirdly, moral sufferings or guilt.

Let us begin with physical sufferings. Our Blessed Lord took upon Himself – it is Matthew who tells us – our sicknesses and our illnesses. Think of that: *He took upon Himself our sicknesses and our illnesses!*[1] Now do we have any record in the Gospel that our Lord was ever sick? No. I do not believe that He ever was sick, because nothing human could ever touch Him until He said the word "now" at the Passion.

For example, they tried to throw Him over the edge of a hill. He walked through the midst of them unharmed. Three times they attempted to stone Him, and He walked away from them. Well, then, if our Lord was never sick, how could it be said that He took upon Himself our sicknesses and our illnesses?

That is not difficult to understand. Many of you good mothers reading this have held your sick infant to

---

1 Cf. Matt 8:17; Is 53:4

your breast, the child being very sick. Because you love that babe, you suffered a thousand times more than your child. If any of you have a delinquent daughter, or any of you men a delinquent son, you suffer more than the delinquent daughter or the delinquent son. Why? On account of your love.

Your suffering, therefore, is not just a sympathy which is outside of us, but rather an empathy which is a deep feeling of the pains of others. Now this is how our Lord transferred to Himself our sicknesses and our illnesses. That is why we read in the Gospels that when our Lord cured the blind, the deaf, and the dumb, what did He do? What does the Gospel tell us was His emotion? The Gospel says He sighed. He groaned. He wept. Three times He wept.[2]

I'm sure that when our Blessed Lord, for example, healed the blind, that all the lights of the world went out for Him. He felt the blindness of a Milton, the deafness of a Beethoven. When He healed leprosy, He felt leprosy inside of Himself, and that was why He gave way to these emotions.[3]

Incidentally, this is the only answer there is to the problem of evil. There is no use in reading books concerning philosophical explanations of evil. The only answer to it is this: That God came into this world and took His own medicine and showed us how to endure and conquer it.

---

2 The editors were only able to find two explicit references to our Lord weeping, John 11:35 and Luke 19:41. The third time may simply be an allusion, which we find in Heb 5:7. There is also the possibility of Mark 15: 27, 34 or 7:34.
3 Cf. Heb 5:7

For example, did God ever have a migraine headache as if His head were crowned with thorns? Does God know anything about the torn flesh of those that are brought into the accident wards of hospitals? Does God know anything about loneliness as if He were abandoned by His most trusted friends? Does God know anything about hunger? Did He ever go without food for three days? Or five days? Does God know anything about thirst?

Yes. God went through all these things in the person of Christ, and all we have to do is walk in His footsteps. But the important point is that He transferred to Himself all our sicknesses and our illnesses.

Next point: He transferred mental ills. Think of, for example, the mentally handicapped people. Mentally retarded children. Agnostics. Scoffers. Doubters. The loneliness of those who had the faith and lost it. Many people in the world are suffering this loneliness, and how could they ever be redeemed unless Christ Himself took all of that mental, existential loneliness upon Himself as if He were guilty of it?

And in one, terrible hour on the cross, when the sun hid its light as if ashamed to shed light upon the crime of deicide, He uttered that shortest of all cries, "My God, My God, why? Why?"[4] It was the moment when God felt atheism. He was at the very brink of hell, and from that time on no one could ever say God does not know anything about despair, about anxiety. Yes, He felt it all. He

---

4 Cf. Matt 27:39; Ps 22:1

transferred it upon Himself.

Thirdly, guilt, which is the most serious of all, and sin. He bore our sins as if He Himself were guilty. He took the punishment which we deserve.[5]

Let me give you this example: Suppose in a courtroom, a judge is seated in judgment. Before him is his own son who committed murder. There is no doubt whatever of the son's guilt. The evidence is in. It is clear. He had murdered a boy, and the boy was buried. Suppose the father, now executing justice, sentences his son to death. That would be justice. But immediately afterwards he steps down from the judge's bench and says to his son, "I will go to death for you." That would be mercy.

Now our Lord does something like that. He says, "All right, I will take your place. You deserve death by your sins. I will take that death upon myself."

But there is something else added. Suppose that immediately after the son had been sentenced to death, the boy who had been murdered walked in alive. What would the condemned youth say? He would say, "How can you condemn me of murder? What evidence have you that I ever killed the boy? Where is the *corpus delicti*?[A] I am innocent! I deserve to be freed."

And he's right, and that's just exactly what happened to us. We are guilty of the death of Christ, and when Christ

---

5 Cf. 2 Cor 5:21

is raised from the dead gloriously on Easter Sunday, we who are guilty of His death can say, "See? See? He's alive! I'm free!"

That's Christianity. That's the complete transference of guilt to Himself and the conquest of it by His Resurrection. Now this is the very heart and soul of Christianity.

But I am here to inform you about the Little Flower in relationship to the gospel. Let me show you now how she is a saint, for every saint, every Christian has to do this. Let me show you how the Little Flower took upon herself first of all the physical ills of the world, secondly, mental, and thirdly, moral.

First of all, she took upon herself the physical ills of the world, and in her writings, what we find is a desire to be a victim. We priests always speak of ourselves as priests. Well, we're not just priests, really. There is a hyphen after that word priest. Because our Lord was not just a priest. A priest is someone who offers something. What did our Lord offer? He offered Himself. He didn't offer a bullock or a goat or a sheep. He offered Himself in sacrifice for us. Therefore, He was Priest–Victim.[B]

So the Little Flower said, "When I enter Carmel, I must become a physical victim for the sins of the world." So she is going to transfer to herself and to her life of penance the sicknesses and the illnesses of others that they might not rebel against God. Here is an excerpt, for example, from many of her words about victimhood:

142

> To offer oneself as a victim to Divine Love is
> not to offer oneself to sweetness and to
> consolation but to every bitterness, for love
> lives only by sacrifice. And the more a soul wills
> to be surrendered to Love, the more must she be
> surrendered to sacrifice.

So as our Blessed Lord, therefore, took upon Himself penances of suffering (going 40 days without food, for example, the scourgings, the pain of crucifixion), the Little Flower transfers to herself the physical deaths that are due to sinners in order that their punishment might be expiated and atoned by her victimhood. This is one of the reasons, incidentally, why we have to have Orders in the Church that will transfer to themselves the penances that we ought to be doing. There are pleasures, *illicit* pleasures which we derive, for which no atonement has been made. So someone has to pay the debt.

Well, that was what the Little Flower said she was doing. She was not in there to save her own soul as the Religious now are not here to save their own souls. And we priests are not. We are to save the souls of others. We are to be victims for Christ's sake, as she was a victim in the physical order, but also in the mental order.

Now as our Blessed Lord took upon Himself the mental sufferings of the world—anguish, loneliness, darkness, as if He were abandoned by God—so the Little Flower had to suffer darkness. You will never find a saint who has not had tremendous mental anguish of one kind or another. St. Teresa the Great of Spain, for example, was

18 years living in a sense that there was no God, that she was abandoned. Was this just for the expiation of her own faults? No! She was transferring to herself the anguish in the depths of others that they might not ever lose their souls. Now here is an example of how the Little Flower took upon herself some sufferings:

> There are souls which have no faith and which lose through the misuse of grace this precious treasure fountain of all pure and true happiness. And now in these happy days of Easter, Jesus taught me to realize that. He allowed my soul to be overrun by an impenetrable darkness which made the thought of heaven hitherto so welcome a subject of nothing but conflict and torment. And this trial was not to be a matter of days or even a few weeks, it was to last until the moment when God should see fit to remove it. And that moment has not come yet.

And that is why those of you who are attending Masses and services in honor of the Little Flower will have in your intention the recovery of faith of those that have lost it, applying the mental sufferings of our Lord and the mental sufferings of the Little Flower to these particular souls.

And finally, moral suffering. Moral guilt! I told you how our Blessed Lord took our sins upon Himself. The Little Flower did the same. One day she heard of a criminal who was to be executed. Actually this criminal had murdered two women and a child. He had committed the murders in the course of a theft and had refused all priestly ministrations. The Little Flower heard all about this criminal. Remember what I told you: There's a price tag on every soul. Someone has to pay the debt in union with the sufferings of our Lord.

She said:

> I had been told about an abandoned wretch who had just been condemned to death for appalling crimes, and there was every reason to think that he would die impenitent. He must be saved from hell. I tried everything. There was nothing I could do myself, but I could offer to God our Lord's infinite merits and all the treasury of the soul of the Church.

> I got my sister Céline to have a Mass said for me. I asked it for myself because I was shy about owning that it was for Pranzini, that wretched criminal. I'd rather not have told Céline, but she questioned me so eagerly and lovingly that I had to tell her. And she didn't make fun of me. On the contrary she wanted to give me her help in converting this sinner. I was only too thankful, and I would have liked all creation to join with me in praying for the grace that was needed. And in my heart I felt certain we would not be disappointed.

> I did ask for a sign. I told God I was sure He meant to pardon that unfortunate Pranzini, and

I had such confidence in our Lord's mercy that
I would cling to my belief even if Pranzini
didn't go to confession but only made some
gesture of repentance. I would like to see some
sign of repentance from him while I offered my
sacrifices for him. Pranzini went to the
guillotine refusing the ministry of the priest. But
the priest accompanied him nevertheless, and
just before the knife fell, he said to the priest,
"The crucifix! The crucifix!" And he kissed it
and went to his death.

Our Lord died for sinners. The Little Flower took on
moral guilt for sinners.

I was in London last week where I visited a nun
whom I brought back to the Church years ago, a woman
who was an actress, and she entered a contemplative
community.[c] And she told me that she had read in the
paper about someone who was to be hanged in Scotland.
And she asked the Mother Superior if the Community
would join in prayers that this man might show some
sign of repentance. Up to that time he had refused. And
the Mother Superior said, "We're already burdened with
petitions, but you make this novena yourself."

So at the beginning of the novena to the Little
Flower, she put a red rose before a statue of the Little
Flower and prayed for nine days. On the ninth day, he was
to be executed. And in the morning when she went to the
statue, all of the petals had fallen off of the rose and were
lying on the floor. And she said, "I took this as a sign that

the Little Flower was letting fall a shower of roses and that the man would make some repentance. It was only two weeks later that I discovered that the man, just before he was hanged, made his act of repentance to God and died in His mercy."

Now to sum it up, our Lord is the model of our spiritual life. He took upon Himself our physical illnesses so that we would not complain but bear them patiently. He took upon Himself all of our mental sufferings so that we would never be discouraged, for He went into the dark for us, Himself alone. Thirdly, He took upon Himself our moral guilt. Now we are, as Christians, to continue the work of Christ. Therefore, we will transfer physically the pains of others to ourselves. The lame, the sick, the blind, we will help in Christ's name. We will transfer their physical handicaps to ourselves. With the mentally handicapped, patience, seeing beyond the merely physical and visible the Christ Whose images they are in, and with a smile and with kindness bringing them the hope of Christ.

And finally, moral guilt. Among most of you (as is usually the case with Christian people), there are those whom we know who have fallen into sin and are unrepentant. Let me tell you that no prayer of yours for the recovery of a soul from sin if persisted in will ever be unheard. It is not necessary always that the great sinner pray for himself. Remember that as St. Paul says, no man dies alone.[6] No man lives alone. Your prayers will save those souls. Remember the paralytic who was let down through

---

6 Cf. Rom 14:7

the roof? He did not ask to be brought to our Lord. He did not ask to have his sins forgiven. He did not ask to be healed. But our Lord forgave his sins, and our Lord healed him. Why? If you read the Gospel carefully, you will find the reason. It was because of the prayers of the four men who let him down through the roof. They prayed for him, and he was healed.[7]

This then is the lesson that the Little Flower will give to you, the lesson of transference following that of the Good Lord Himself. And in the next chapter, I will discuss how the Little Flower handled handicaps, difficulties, trials, and disappointments, and about a special devotion she had to the Precious Blood of our Blessed Lord.

---

7 Cf. Mark 2:1-12

∽❧❧

Notes

A. *Corpus delicti* is Latin for "the body of the offense; the essence of the crime." According to one online source, it is "a general rule not to convict unless the *corpus delicti* can be established, that is, until the dead body has been found. Instances have occurred of a person being convicted of having killed another, who, after the supposed criminal has been put to death for the supposed offence, has made his appearance alive."

B. Cf. *CCC* 1586. For a beautiful meditation on the nature of the priest as victim, see the essay on this subject by Msgr. Arthur B. Calkins titled, "Padre Pio: Priest and Victim." http://www.piercedhearts.org/theology_heart/padre_pio_priest_victim.htm. See also "Jesus Christ: Priest and Victim," *The Voice of Padre Pio* XXVI, No. 1 (January 1996) 5-15 [a conference given in San Giovanni Rotondo, 9 October 1995], which quotes Archbishop Sheen extensively on the idea of priest as victim. You will also find same thought in Sheen's own book *The Priest is Not His Own.*

C. Who was this woman? No one knows for certain. All we know is she became Sr. Tarcissius (or maybe Tarcissus), a Benedictine nun at the Tyburn Convent in London, and served there for some 40 years. As Fr. John Hardon, SJ, wrote, "Fulton Sheen's interest in converting non-Catholics and bringing lapsed Catholics back to the

Church dates from his earliest years in the priesthood. With his increased popularity as a speaker and writer, requests for instruction multiplied from prospective converts – with remarkable success. Senator Wagner, the champion of labor; Heywood Broun, columnist and freethinker; Gretta Palmer, the writer; Fritz Kreisler, violinist [who went on to write the theme song for Sheen's TV show; for his fascinating and brief conversion story, read Sheen's autobiography, *A Treasure in Clay*]; Elizabeth Bentley, communist underground worker; Henry Ford II, the motor industrialist, are some of the 'notables' whom Bishop (as Father and Monsignor) Sheen brought to the Catholic Faith. But there have been hundreds of obscure converts too: the English actress who later became a contemplative nun [her compelling story is also in the archbishop's autobiography]; the French woman on the verge of suicide whom he saved and turned into a daily communicant; the Jewish girl, cast off by her family for becoming a Catholic, whom he set up in a beauty shop; the bigot who approached him to abuse him, and who ended as a zealous lay apostle for the faith."

CHAPTER 10

St. Thérèse and humility, the way of the child

Up to this point in the *triduum*[A] of the Little Flower I have not told you anything about her humility. As I mentioned before, some call it the Little Way, but it is not little in the sense of easy. As a matter of fact, it is very difficult to be humble.

For example, some people say, "Oh, I was never meant for great things."

That is not humility. That is indifference. It would not be humility for a man who is 6'5" tall to say, "Oh, I'm only 5'4"." That is not humility. Humility is truth.

Now the Little Flower was once asked, "What do you mean and understand by humility and the way of the child?" I'm going to give you her answer. Then I'm going to explain it. This is the way she explained in answer to the question on childhood:

> To remain little is to recognize our
> nothingness.

Now that's the point I want to emphasize. It might be even just enough to read this line. Read it again…

> *To remain little is to recognize our nothingness.*

> To expect everything from the good God and
> not to be too much afflicted about our faults,
> for little children fall often but are too small to
> hurt themselves.

In other words, the way of humility is the way of nothingness. I could not find in the writings of the Little Flower that she ever quoted St. Paul in this connection, because he also said our Lord made Himself nothing. However, isn't it interesting that she should use the same word that St. Paul used to describe the Incarnation of our Blessed Lord?[1]

Did you ever really sit down and think out what it meant for God to become man? Sometime try to picture that, God making Himself nothing.

The most beautiful passage about nothingness is in St. Paul's Letter to the Philippians. Now it is not an easy text, but suffer with me as I share it, and then I'll give you an explanation you can readily understand. This is in the second chapter of St. Paul's Letter to the Philippians. He

---

1 Cf. Phil 2:7

said:

> Let your bearing toward one another arise out
> of your life in Christ Jesus. For the Divine
> Nature was His from the first ...

What does that mean? That meant that Christ was
always God. The Divine Nature was always His. Now the
next line:

> ... yet He did not think to snatch at equality
> with God.

Whoever tried "to snatch at equality with God"?
Satan. *He* tried to make himself God. Who else? Adam.
Satan told Adam that he would become like God. Now
He Who really was God, Christ, does not try to snatch at
equality with God as Satan did and as Adam did. Now we
come to the phrase:

> But He made Himself nothing, nothing,
> assuming the nature of a slave.[2]

Slave. Not servant. Slave. What does a slave do? Two
kinds of work: Dirty work and hard work. So our Lord,
therefore, made Himself nothing when He became man.
The Little Flower says:

> The secret of spiritual childhood is to make
> yourself nothing.

---

2 Phil 2:5-7

I wish she had quoted that text. It would have helped us understand. But I am going to explain it even more simply. It is not easy for us to understand this descent from the glory of God down to the frailty of the human nature by our Blessed Lord becoming a slave. That word "slave" is used in the gospels and the epistles 44 times about our Lord when He made Himself nothing.

Now, for example, suppose that you were very much concerned about the way dogs acted in Dublin. I hope I'm not maligning the dogs, but suppose that the dogs in Dublin never obeyed their masters. They snapped at children. They barked at postmen. They refused to be housebroken.

I was in the Carmelite Convent where they had a little dog, and despite all the good example of those Sisters, they held the dog when I was there. They said, "Oh, the little dog might snap at you." So there are bad dogs in Dublin, you see!

Now suppose you were distressed at the way dogs acted in Dublin, and you wanted to make dogs good and obedient. Suppose, furthermore, that to do this you took off, you gave up, you surrendered your body. Suppose you had that power, and all you kept was your mind, your spirit, and you would put your mind into the body of a dog.

For the purpose of teaching dogs to be good, just to follow our example, you would be reduced to nothingness in two kinds of ways. First of all, though you knew you could speak, you would only bark. Though you knew that you had reason which could scan the stars, you would follow instinct. And the other humiliation, which you would have as a result of putting your mind into the body of a dog would be this: You would have to spend the rest of your life with dogs! Running with them, doing the things that they did, knowing all the while that you were a thousand times better.

And then suppose at the end, the dogs, instead of learning from you, they turned on you and tore you to pieces.

Well, if you would find that very humbling, to take on the body of a dog and live with dogs, what do you think it was for God to become man and take upon Himself our human nature?

First of all, He is the Word of God, and now, because He takes on our human nature, He talks in words.

Secondly, He has to spend His life with stupid men. And stupid they were. For example, the night of the Last Supper, Thomas heckles Him.[3] So does Philip. And our Lord has to say to Philip, "Oh, Philip. Philip, have I been with you all this time and still you do not understand?"[4]

And then in the end we throw our Lord out of the city and crucify Him. This is what is meant by God becoming nothing, becoming even a slave. Not only in order to teach us to be good but to redeem us from our sins.

---

3 Cf. John 14:5
4 Cf. John 14:9

Coming back now to the Little Flower. What is the secret of humility? She said it is to become nothing. Nothing. Never to stress our own powers, our own wealth (if we have any), our own gifts, but to recognize they all come from God.

There are two kinds of emptiness. There is the emptiness of the Grand Canyon in the United States; it is sterile and produces nothing. There is also the emptiness of a flute, which if you breathe through, you can pipe a tune. Now we are bidden, like our Blessed Lord, to become empty, to become nothing so He can work on us. That is the basis of humility. That is what people called her Little Way.

Now take, for example, myself. I have the power of preaching. When I talk to you, you listen. Is this any power of my own? Should I boast of it? No, I'm merely using a gift God gave me. As St. Paul says, "What is it that you have that you have not received? And if you have received, why do you glory as if you had not?"[5]

So I have to thank Him every day for this gift.

Humility, therefore, means recognizing the gifts that we have. I often think of the young people today who make millions on their records. Their music is not great, but at any rate it is popularized, advertised (and sometimes very artificially), but as a result, fortunes are made. I wonder if they ever thank God for any voice that they do have

---

5 1 Cor 4:7

and if they ever thank God for the money that they have received?

So humility, therefore, is a recognition of dependence and littleness, and it is this that made the Little Flower a saint. She never boasted of anything she could do. As a matter of fact, she welcomed humiliations. And it's interesting that she knew the story of Shimei, because not many people do. I had occasion once to use it in a conversation with Pope John.[B]

King David was out one day on campaign, and Shimei attacked him and said all manner of evil things against King David. And one of David's generals said to him, "Shall I take out my sword and kill him?"

David said, "No. God made him to humble me, to make me little."[6]

I've had those in my life, too, who were made to humble me. The Little Flower went out of her way to get people to humble her. And she would often thank God for any humiliation she might have. Our modern world, you see, has gotten so far away from this idea, that if anything wrong is done, they immediately want to excuse or exonerate themselves with never an admission of guilt.

This then is, as simply as I can put it, the story of becoming nothing as our Lord did. If you have a box that is filled with salt, you cannot fill it with pepper, can you?

---

6 Cf. 2 Sam 16:5-14

Well, if we are filled with our own self and our own ego, God can't get in! We often wonder, for example, why it is that there is no room for God in certain hearts. He can't get in! There's no vacancy. But the more empty we are, the more He can fill us with His grace. As a matter of fact, we were made from nothingness, and only when we get back close again to nothingness do we ever get to God.

Remember the woman in the Old Testament who had two sons who were to be sold to creditors, and the prophet Elijah called on her and asked her what she had. She said, "I don't have anything except a small vessel of oil."

And Elijah said, "Tell your sons to go out into the neighborhood, gather up all of the vessels that there are and bring them here."

So the sons hurried out and brought in all kinds of pots and vessels and crocks and the like, and Elijah said to the woman, "Now take your little vessel of oil and start pouring it."

So the woman started pouring the oil into one of the vessels, and the oil didn't stop! And she went from one vessel to the next, to the next, to the next, and so on and so forth. Finally she said to one of her sons, "Give me yet another vessel."

And the son said, "There is no other." And the oil

stopped.[7]

The oil is the Spirit of Christ, and as long as we're empty, God can fill us. And this is what is known as the Little Way, the way of spiritual childhood. Never taking pride in anything we do but referring it to the Good Lord, and if there is any humiliation, referring it to the cross.

And so, my good friends, I have brought you today back to nothingness as our Lord made Himself a zero when He became man. Think of it. A babe in a cradle whose tiny hands were not quite large enough to touch the huge heads of the cattle, and yet He was the one that steers the sun and moon and stars in their courses. This was the humility of Christ. We now know the humility of the Little Flower, and we have only now to practice it ourselves.

꿏

Notes

A.   *Triduum* is Latin for "three days." According to the online *Catholic Encyclopedia*, a *triduum* is "A time frequently chosen for prayer or for other devout practices, whether by individuals in private, or in public by congregations or special organizations in parishes, in religious communities, seminaries, or schools. The form of prayer or devotion depends upon the occasion or purpose of the *triduum*. The

---

7 Cf. 2 Kings 4:1-6

three days usually precede some feast, and the feast then determines the choice of the pious exercises."

B.   This would, of course, be Bl. John XXIII (1958–63), the Pope who called and opened the Second Vatican Council, which lasted from 1962-65, and who was good friends with Sheen.

John may be the only pontiff in the papacy's history to have served during a war as a non-commissioned officer. Shortly after World War I had broken out, Fr. Angelo Roncalli (John's given name) was drafted into the Royal Italian Army. He served for the war's duration as a medical corpsman and a chaplain.

In 1921, Benedict XV made him Italian president of the Society for the Propagation of the Faith, so he and Sheen had a love for missions in common.

Roncalli went on to serve as papal nuncio in several countries, including France and Turkey, in which capacity he helped save thousands of Jews from the concentration camps during World War II.

Pius XII later made him patriarch of Venice, which distinction earned him a place in the college of cardinals.

Because of his open manner, clever sense of humor, and ever-present smile, he became known after his elevation to the papacy as "Good Pope John." He was once asked how many people worked in the Vatican. "About half," he replied. At another time, he joked to Sheen, "God knew from all eternity that I was destined to be Pope. He also knew that I would live for over eighty years. Having all eternity to work on, and also eighty years, wouldn't you think He would have made me better looking?" On yet another occasion, he called the papal photographer to capture a photo of him and Sheen, saying, "Come, let us have our picture taken. It may make some in the Church jealous, but that will be fun."

CHAPTER 11

St. Thérèse, sin, and mercy

We are living in about the only period of the world's history which has denied human guilt and sin. It used to be that we Catholics were the only ones who believed in the Immaculate Conception. Today most people in the world believe they were immaculately conceived, for they deny that there is any such thing as sin or guilt. Dostoevsky, the Russian novelist in the 1800s foretold this condition. He said, "The day is coming when men will say there is no sin, there is no guilt, there is only hunger. And they will come crying and fawning at our feet saying, 'Give us bread.'"[A]

What are the two escapes from human guilt today? The first is people deny they are guilty. They claim they are only sick. Hence there are very few penitents in the world. There are many patients. Just as soon as there is an abnormal manifestation of guilt, they are told that there is no guilt. Now this is not true. A very normal guilt can be at the basis of any abnormal manifestation of guilt. Take for example Shakespeare's tragedy, *Macbeth*. Macbeth and his wife Lady Macbeth contrived to murder the king in order to seize the throne. They both suffered abnormalities after the murder.

Now Shakespeare was born in 1564, long before we had psychiatry, yet he depicted the psychosis in Macbeth and a neurosis in Lady Macbeth. After the crime, Macbeth was constantly seeing before him the dagger with the handle toward his hand. There was no dagger. This was just an abnormal sign of a very normal guilt—murder. And Lady Macbeth washed her hands every quarter of an hour. She thought she saw spots of blood on her hands. There was no blood there. And she said at one moment, "Are not all the waters of the seven seas enough to wash this blood incarnadine from my hands?"[B]

These were the exceptional and extraordinary manifestations of a hidden guilt. Now today when there is a hidden (I mean an abnormal) manifestation of guilt, there is often a denial of real guilt. That is the first escape today.

And the second is we rationalize our sins. We find reasons for them in order to excuse our guilt. We like to get into discussions. Have you ever noticed how often people who fall away from the faith want to discuss it? Religion, really, is a matter of decision, not a matter of discussion.

Remember the time our Lord met the woman at the well? She was a Samaritan woman, and the Jews and the Samaritans never spoke. But our Lord spoke to her. She was rather nasty at first, then became a little nicer as time went on. And our Blessed Lord tried to explain to her the subject of grace. He did it under the analogy of water because she was there at the well to take water. But the woman did not understand what our Lord was saying. Then our Lord said to her, "Go, call your husband, and come here."

She said, "I have no husband."

Our Lord said, "You have said well that you have no husband, for you have had five husbands, and he with whom you live now is not your husband."[1]

See, our Blessed Lord was putting His finger on her adultery and guilt. What did she do? She said, "Let's have a discussion, a theological discussion. Where should we worship, here on this mountain as we Samaritans do, or in the temple of Jerusalem as do the Jews?" Our Blessed Lord eventually brought her to grace, but the point is, you see, she was trying to escape the fact of guilt by getting into a theological discussion and not purifying her soul.

These are the two ways we try to get away from sin today. But sin is the most real thing in the world, and we are all sinners.

I think I told you that I sometimes go to prisons and talk to prisoners. Well, when you stand up before 1,979 inmates of a prison, how do you start? What do you say to them? Everything depends upon how you start. This is the way I start: "Gentlemen, I want you to know there's one

---

1 John 4:7-42

great difference between you and me: You got caught, I didn't. " In other words, we're all sinners.

All right, now admitting the *fact* of guilt, how are sins forgiven? I mean, what is the ultimate ground and basis for the forgiveness of sins? What is necessary before a sin can be committed? Not just your sin and my sin, but all sins of the world? What is the absolute condition? Now the reason I've chosen this subject is because the Little Flower knew, and we ought to know, too. Now think in your own minds: What do you think is the basis for the forgiveness of sins? I'm going to give you the answer from Scripture. It's in the ninth chapter of the Hebrews:

> Without the shedding of blood, there is no forgiveness of sin.[2]

Think of that! Without the shedding of blood, there is no forgiveness of sin. Why is the shedding of blood necessary? Well, first of all, because sin is in the blood. It's in the blood of the addict. It's in the blood of the alcoholic. It's in the blood of the degenerate. And somehow or other, if sin is ever to be forgiven, blood has to be poured out. And furthermore, sin is such a serious offense that it takes the blood of someone to block out its terrible burden. So the condition of forgiving sin, therefore, is the shedding of blood.

The Little Flower was unconsciously a great theologian. She knew this. And she very often, when she

---

2 Heb 9:22

prayed for sinners, would invoke the blood of Christ. For example:

> The Precious Blood of Jesus I poured
> on souls.

She said she bemoaned that more people were not receiving a drop of the Blood of Christ. In her story of the conversion of the criminal Pranzini, whom I discussed earlier, he had killed two women and a child, and he was to be guillotined. The Little Flower heard about him refusing to acknowledge he had been a sinner, and she prayed for him. And just before he was executed at the guillotine, he said to the priest, "The crucifix! The crucifix!" And he kissed it three times. The Little Flower tells that story. And then she says, addressing the Reverend Mother:

> My victory is always to run away from evil. But
> for the conversion of souls, there must be the
> sight of the Precious Blood flowing from our
> Lord's wounds. And this is to be the cordial
> bond that will heal all their sins.

In other words, the Little Flower is a theologian. She is saying just exactly what the Scripture says. There has to be the shedding of blood before there can be forgiveness of sins.

Now let me take you on a tour, a tour of Scripture, to show you how right the Little Flower is and the great mystery of the Precious Blood.

When our first parents sinned, they perceived themselves to be naked. Why naked? Well, because they had already been clothed with an aura of grace. And when they lost that grace then they perceived themselves to be naked. They covered up their nakedness with fig leaves. Shame is exposure. The fig leaves dried and again they were in shame. How did they cover up their shame? Now this is the test of how well you know Scripture. And I hope I send you back to your Bibles to do some reading.

It's in the third chapter of the book of Genesis. How was their shame covered up? "God made for them the skins of animals."[3] That's right. *God made for them the skins of animals.* In order to have the skin of an animal, there had to be the shedding of blood. God did not kill Adam and Eve. He killed a substitute, an animal. Note, therefore, that God first does something. Second, it involves the shedding of blood. And, third, a substitute is used. In other words, an animal was killed instead of Adam and Eve.

Now this truth of the shedding of blood being the foundation of the expiation of sins we find immediately with Cain. Cain killed Abel. Because he *murdered*, he was afraid of *being* murdered.[4] And God said all right I will put a sign on you which will protect you from being murdered. What was the sign? We do not know exactly, but I think it was the blood of his brother Abel. For without the shedding of blood there is no remission of sin.

Now we come to Abraham, and he is told by God to

---

3 Gen 3:17
4 Cf. Gen 4:15

166

sacrifice his son. Can you imagine that?! He waited until he was almost 100 to have a son. Then when he has a son, God says, "Now offer him up in sacrifice." Well, Abraham was very obedient. He put wood on the back of his son Isaac, and for three days Isaac by intention was dead because he was under the sentence of death. Cannot you see here the picture of the heavenly Father laying wood on the back of His Son and climbing up Mount Calvary?

So when finally Abraham after three days takes his son to the mount, the son says to the father, "Where is the lamb?" Where is the lamb? And those words were caught up on the top of Mount Moriah, and they rang down through the centuries. Where is the lamb? Where is the lamb? The father said, "God will provide." And at that moment when he held the knife above his son's neck, the angel stayed the knife. And there was a ram that was found in the bushes nearby, and the ram was sacrificed in place of the son, Isaac.[5] God does something. He does it vicariously or by a substitute, namely the ram, and thirdly, it involved the shedding of blood.

Now we come to Moses. Moses is in Egypt with the Israelites. God had worked many wonders for Moses against Pharaoh, the king of the Egyptians. And Moses after each miracle had begged Pharaoh let his people go. Pharaoh would promise and then recant. And finally God said to Moses, "Tonight I will kill the firstborn of man and beast in all of Egypt. But Moses, you take a lamb, kill it, take the blood of that lamb, and sprinkle it over the top of

---

5 Cf. Gen 22:7-13

your doors."

Not on the floor. Blood is sacred. The Jewish people were not allowed to touch blood in food that belonged to God.

"So take the blood, sprinkle it over the doorposts... And when the angel [sic] that destroys the first born of man and beast that night passes through the city, he will see the blood and pass over that house."[6]

That is the origin of the Passover. God did something. Two, it was done through a substitute, a lamb. And thirdly, it involved the shedding of blood. And that is how the firstborn of all of the Jews were saved whereas the firstborn of all the Egyptians were lost.

From that time on Moses now offers the paschal lamb. Paschal lamb means the Passover lamb. And the Jewish people had to eat it standing, loins girt, carrying a staff. We are pilgrims. We have no lasting city here.

As the Passover continued, Moses now acting as God's representative, gave further explanation to the mystery of blood. One of them was the scapegoat. On the day of atonement, two goats were brought before the high priest. One goat was to be killed. The one to be killed was chosen by lot. "Which of the two do you wish me to release to you? Christ or Barabbas?"[7]

---

6 Cf. Ex 12:7-13
7 Cf. Matt 27:17

The blood of the goat that was killed was then sprinkled on the other goat. But the priest would first lay his hands over that goat just the same as the priest does at Mass. You know, just before the Consecration we lay our hands over the Host and the chalice. Well, that is what the Jewish priest did. He was laying the sins of all of the Jewish people on that goat.[c] And laden with sins then, he was sprinkled with blood, which brought forgiveness. And the scapegoat was led by a Gentile out 60 or 70 miles away and thrown over a precipice. And the Jews then said, "Well, all of our sins are carried away." Sins are forgiven by the shedding of blood.

There are many other symbols, but I will quickly pass over the story of blood with just one more symbol from the Old Testament.

When the Israelites in crossing the desert disobeyed God, they were bitten by serpents. And God said to Moses, "Make a serpent of brass. Hang that brass serpent up on the crotch of a tree and everyone who looks on that serpent of brass will be healed of the poisonous bite of the snake."[8]

Now there's nothing in looking at a brass serpent that will cure a snake bite. Nothing. But these things were done to prefigure of our Lord's coming.

And here I jump quickly to our Lord, but I will come back to the Old Testament history. Remember when our Lord was visited at night by Nicodemus (and

---

8 Cf. Numb 21:6-9

he appears in the Gospel only at night; you never see him in the daytime)? Our Lord said to Nicodemus, "As Moses lifted up the serpent in the desert so must the Son of Man be lifted up on the cross."[9]

In other words, our Lord is calling Himself that brass serpent. And this was the meaning: That serpent of brass had no poison in it. But it looked exactly like the serpent that did bite them and gave them poison. All who with faith looked on that serpent of brass in the desert were healed. Now our Lord said, "I am that serpent of brass. When I am hung up on the crotch of a tree, of the cross, I will look as if I am full of the poison of sin! But there is no more sin in me than there was poison in that serpent of brass. And all who look upon Me will be healed."

That was the meaning of the brass serpent.

Now we come to the New Testament and the first Passover of our Lord's public life. Remember the scene: John the Baptist is preaching at the Jordan; it's time for all of the Jewish people to bring their lambs to the Temple to be sacrificed. And we know from a first century authority that the Jews offered as many as 260,000 lambs in the Temple. The Jewish religion was a veritable hemorrhage of blood.

Well, John the Baptist, as he's preaching along the Jordan, looks out on this road that leads across the Jordan to Jericho and then up to the city of Jerusalem. Hundreds of thousands of pilgrims. Every family had to have a paschal

---

9 John 3:14

lamb. If they were poor, 20 people could unite and buy a lamb.

John the Baptist looks out at this procession, some of the children carrying the lambs. Other lambs had red ribbons, scarlet ribbons, purple ribbons about their neck, destined for sacrifice. And all the while, the Jewish people who had been offering the paschal lamb in sacrifice, had remembered the words of Isaac on the mount 1,500, 1,700 years before: "Where is the lamb?" Where is the lamb?

And as John the Baptist looked at all of them, he suddenly spotted someone in the crowd, and he said, "There's the Lamb!! *The Lamb of God* Who takes away the sin of the world."[10]

The Lamb had come. It was Christ. "Where is the lamb?" And that's the reason the Jews no longer have sacrifice of lambs in their Temple: The Lamb has come.

Three years later, God does something. He sends His Son. Two, He saves us by a substitute: Christ dies in our place. And thirdly, our redemption from sin involved the shedding of the Blood of Christ.

This is our faith. Every time you go to confession, whenever a priest raises his hand in absolution over your sins, the Blood of Christ is dripping from his fingers. When you receive Communion, you are receiving the Body and Blood of Christ. Moses used to take the blood of the lamb

---

10 John 1:29

and sprinkle the congregation with it as we sprinkle it with holy water. In receiving Communion, you are sprinkled with the Blood of Christ.

That was what the Little Flower invoked when she prayed for the conversion of Pranzini, that the Blood of Christ be on his soul. This is what you must invoke after a sin or a fault, the Blood of Christ. This then is the basis of forgiveness.

Now as our Lord was dying on the cross, we must recall a scene. We go into the city of Jerusalem. Our Lord was crucified outside of the city. That was where the blood victims had to be thrown according to Jewish law. And so the true Blood Victim is thrown outside of the city. In the Temple of Jerusalem, there is a great veil of hyacinth, gold, purple, red, crimson, 60 feet high. And sewn into the veil, two tremendous cherubim, which St. Peter says are always gazing at the mystery of redemption. That is why we should always have at the altar two cherubim on either side of the Tabernacle.

But coming back now to this Temple. It's the Day of Atonement.[D] The Jews are preparing for the high priest to enter into that veil. He may do it only once a year. So the high priest dips his hyssop in blood. And he sprinkles that veil, which gives him the right to enter the Holy of Holies.

Just at that moment the side of Christ was pierced with a lance, and this veil in the Temple was ripped not from bottom to top – for a man could do that – but from

172

top to bottom. And the Holy of Holies, which only the high priest could ever see (and only once a year), now was exposed to everyone. And when the heart, the veil of Christ's flesh was rent, the true Holy of Holies, heaven itself, was opened. It was no longer hidden behind a veil. Redemption had been completed. The Blood of Christ had been shed. We have been saved. And this beautiful mystery we read again in the epistle of the Hebrews in the chapter just succeeding the one where we read, "without the shedding of blood, there is no forgiveness."[11]

So now, my friends, the Blood of Jesus makes us free to boldly enter into the sanctuary, the Sanctuary of Heaven, by the new living way which He has opened for us through the curtain which is His Flesh. In other words, this curtain in the Temple was only the symbol of Christ's flesh. The priest by sprinkling that curtain could enter into the Holy of Holies, but by the rending of the flesh of Christ, the real curtain which veiled heaven is now open. So we have a great Priest set over the Household of God. And let us make our approach in sincerity of heart and with full assurance of faith, our guilty hearts sprinkled clean, our bodies washed with pure water.

And this, my friends, is the story of how sin is forgiven. And I believe that as we cease to invoke the Blood of Christ for our sins, there is nevertheless in the subconscious of the human race a strong understanding that, somehow or other, blood is necessary for the purification of sin. When we do not invoke the Blood of Christ to have our sins

---

11 Heb 9:22

173

forgiven, we begin to shed one another's blood in the dirty business of war.

Our frail little Thérèse, who claimed not to have any deep knowledge, was a deeper theologian than many of us. For she understood this mystery I have expounded to you, and I've saved this meditation for the end that you might understand the grandeur and the importance of it. Let no one, therefore, ever despair of mercy. The Blood of Christ has paid *all* debts *if you but invoke it.* And who else can ever help us anyway?

As the Hound of Heaven said to us in Francis Thompson's poem,

> Strange, piteous futile thing!
>> Wherefore should any set thee love apart?
> Seeing none but I make not much of naught, He said.
>> And human love needs human meriting.
> How hast thou merited
>> Of all man's clotted clay, the dingiest clot?
> Alack, thou knowest not
>> How little worthy of any love thou art!
> Whom wilt thou find to love ignoble thee,
>> Save Me, save only Me?
> All which I took from thee I did but take,
>> Not for thy harms,
> But just that thou might'st seek it in My arms?
>> All which thy child's mistake
> Fancies as lost, I have stored for thee at home:
>> Rise, clasp My hand, and come!

❧

Notes

A. "Dost Thou know that the ages will pass, and humanity will proclaim by the lips of their sages that there is no crime, and therefore no sin; there is only hunger? 'Feed men, and then ask of them virtue!' ... No science will give them bread so long as they remain free. In the end they will lay their freedom at our feet, and say to us, 'Make us your slaves, but feed us.' They will understand themselves, at last, that freedom and bread enough for all are inconceivable together, for never, never will they be able to share between them" *The Brothers Karamazov*, Fyodor Dostoevsky, Chapter 36.

B. This was actually spoken by the character Macbeth in Act II, Scene II, 68-73.

C. See Lev 16:21

D. This is better known to most people as Yom Kippur.

⟨∾⟩

Prayer for the Canonization of the Servant of God Archbishop Fulton J. Sheen

Heavenly Father, source of all holiness, You raise up within the Church at every age men and women who serve with heroic love and dedication. You have blessed Your Church through the life and ministry of Your faithful servant Archbishop Fulton J. Sheen. He has written and spoken well of Your Divine Son Jesus Christ and was a true instrument of the Holy Spirit in teaching the hearts of countless people.

If it be according to Your will for the honor and glory of the Most Holy Trinity and for the salvation of souls, we ask You to move the Church to proclaim him a saint. We ask this prayer through Jesus Christ our Lord. Amen.

Prayer to Obtain a Favor Through the Intercession of the Servant of God Archbishop Fulton J. Sheen

Eternal Father, You alone grant us every blessing in heaven and on earth through the redemptive mission of Your Divine Son Jesus Christ and by the working of the Holy Spirit.

If it be according to Your will, glorify Your servant

Archbishop Fulton J. Sheen by granting the favor I now request through his prayerful intercession (mention your request).

I make this prayer confidently through Jesus Christ our Lord. Amen.

Morning Prayer of St. Thérèse

O my God! I offer Thee all my actions of this day for the intentions and for the glory of the Sacred Heart of Jesus. I desire to sanctify every beat of my heart, my every thought, my simplest works, by uniting them to Its infinite merits; and I wish to make reparation for my sins by casting them into the furnace of Its Merciful Love.

O my God! I ask of Thee for myself and for those whom I hold dear the grace to perfectly fulfill Thy Holy Will, to accept for love of Thee the joys and sorrows of this passing life, so that we may one day be united together in heaven for all Eternity. Amen.

Miraculous Prayer for the Intervention of St. Thérèse

O glorious St. Thérèse, whom Almighty God has raised up to aid and counsel mankind, I implore your Miraculous Intercession. So powerful are you in obtaining every need of body and soul that our Holy Mother Church proclaims you a "Prodigy of Miracles . . . the Greatest Saint of Modern Times." Now I fervently beseech you to answer my petition [describe your petition here] and to carry out your promises of spending Heaven doing good on earth . . . of letting fall from Heaven a Shower of Roses. Henceforth, dear Little Flower, I will fulfill your plea "to be made known everywhere," and I will never cease to lead others to Jesus through you. Amen.

෧෨෩ඏ

Archbishop Fulton John Sheen Foundation

Formed in 1998, the Archbishop Fulton John Sheen Foundation functions as the "promoter of the Cause" for the canonization of the late Archbishop Fulton J. Sheen. One of its roles is the gathering of information about the life, virtues, and apostolic works of Archbishop Sheen. This is done primarily through contact with people who knew the archbishop personally and so can testify as witnesses to his sanctity. The Foundation must also oversee a critical theological review of all of the archbishop's writings.

The Foundation has already been involved in this work since canon law requires that for a bishop to petition that a cause be opened, he must have sufficient proof that the candidate for sainthood possesses a true and widespread reputation for two important qualities.

The first is a "reputation for holiness." This means that the People of God, especially those who knew that candidate for sainthood personally, genuinely esteemed him or her to have been a saintly person.

The second is a "reputation for intercessory power." This means that people who have prayed to God through the intercession of the candidate for sainthood have received real physical or spiritual favors as a result, such as a healing of illness, help through a personal or family crisis, a personal conversion, or the conversion of a loved one, and the like. The Foundation was already able to offer some of this proof to Bishop Daniel Jenky, CSC, of Peoria to move him to open the Cause.

If you are interested in helping move Archbishop Sheen's cause forward, here are some ways you can help:

1. Pray for favors obtained through Archbishop Sheen's intercession.
2. Notify the Archbishop Sheen Foundation about favors received.
3. Contact the Foundation with personal testimony about the archbishop's life and virtues.
4. Become a member of "The Prayer League of the Friends of Archbishop Fulton J. Sheen." See www.ArchbishopSheenCause.org for more information.
5. Support the Wartime Prayer Book Campaign. See www.ArchbishopSheenCause.org for more information.
6. Become a benefactor. See www.ArchbishopSheenCause.org for more information.

*Archbishop Sheen's Final Farewell**

*Our Lord came to this earth to experience
What it is like when we are disappointed....*

> *At not getting a hotel reservation;
> At having to bump up against so many stubborn
> donkeys and dumb oxen on our way
> through life;
> For not getting the Birthday gifts we
> expected...*

*BUT. He also came to teach us we would never
be disappointed...*

> *If we found that Love we fall just
> short of in all loves;*

> *If we learn to see that, next to His Presence
> in the Blessed Sacrament, our
> neighbor is the most Christ-like
> object we will ever know;*

> *And if we learn to admit the dirt in the
> stable of our own lives,
> We will have found the first sign
> of His Presence in us...*

> *Then we will understand that if He relieved
> us of every disappointment;
> If He gave us only nice, new things;*

*We might forget HIM
And that would rob us of the joy of
Wishing one another*

Merry Christmas

Fulton Sheen

---

*This was the Archbishop's final greeting, sent three days before he died. Fr. Linus heard of his friend's death and then received this greeting two days later, signed in his own hand. A beautiful farewell...